THE NEW DICTIONARY
OF
EXISTENTIALISM

THE NEW DICTIONARY OF

EXISTENTIALISM

by
ST. ELMO NAUMAN, JR.

PHILOSOPHICAL LIBRARY

New York

Library of Congress Catalog Card No. 78-118311
SBN 8022-2346-X

Printed in the United States of America

INTRODUCTION

Existentialism is a technical philosophy of wide influence and of considerable depth. The number of technical terms which it employs must be precisely defined in order that the intended thought may be properly understood. *The New Dictionary of Existentialism* is designed to provide such definitions based on the documentary source materials by major existentialists, such as Kierkegaard, Nietzsche, Sartre, Jaspers, Marcel, Heidegger, Camus, and Berdyaev.

The material contained in this dictionary is limited to the major existentialists in the philosophical and psychological fields. The literary existentialists, while consulted, are treated as secondary to the philosophical formulations of existentialism. In the case of Sartre, however, whenever his philosophical concepts are contained in his literary works, the relevant passages have been included as a primary source for the definition required.

Existentialism is viewed as a philosophy which had its inception at a relatively recent point in time, specifically, in the thought and work of Søren Kierkegaard (1813-1855). Whatever historical antecedents there may have been, variously listed as including Pascal, Socrates, and St. Paul, are not considered directly relevant to this study.

Some recent thinkers, such as Paul Tillich, may or may not be classed as proper existentialists. Nevertheless, their comments and judgments have been included because of their extraordinary value in providing perspective on the movement as a whole.

A

ABSTRACTION: (Latin *ab*, from + *trahere*, to remove)

Existentialists criticize idealistic philosophy for its abstract character, for having abstracted thought from life. Believing that no definition of reality can substitute for reality itself, existentialists seek to avoid such abstraction. They oppose what they call "abstract thought" and attempt to keep thought as "existential" as possible, which is to say, as full of emotion and actual life as possible.

Secondarily, existential thinkers recommend abstraction as a kind of synonym for "reflection," that is, as the opposite of an entirely unreflective life, a life lived on the sensual level of pleasure.

1. The abstract problem of reality (if it is permissible to treat this problem abstractly, the particular and the accidental being constituents of the real, and directly opposed to abstraction) is not nearly so difficult a problem as it is to raise and to answer the question of what it means that this definite something is a reality. This definite something is just what abstract thought abstracts from. But the difficulty lies in bringing this definite something and the ideality of thought together, by penetrating the concrete particularity with thought. Abstract thought cannot even take cognizance of this contradiction, since the very process of abstraction prevents the contradiction from arising. — Søren Kierkegaard, *Concluding Unscientific Postscript,* 267.

2. All wisdom of life is abstraction, and only the most wretched eudaemonism has no abstraction, but is sheer

1

enjoyment of the moment. In the degree to which a eudaemo-nistic philosophy of life is prudent it has some abstraction; the more prudence the more abstraction. — Kierkegaard, *Concluding Unscientific Postscript*, 381n.

3. Karl Jaspers writes that the correct degree of abstraction is that necessary to prevent blind attachment to hedonism or utopianism. These two incorrect beliefs are sunk in the empirical world, the world of "being-there." Yet too great a degree of abstraction, such as is the case with the spectator or the mystic, who completely disengages himself from the empirical world, is equally mistaken. Such an abstraction is not raising oneself above the world, but merely failing to become oneself. When the correct degree of abstraction is attained, the individual will engage himself in the tasks of the world, accepting life without illusion, accepting conflict, suffering, death, but able to go forward with hope.

See also: Being; Existence.

ABSURD: (Latin *absurdus*, not to be heard of)

The absurd is viewed either (as with Kierkegaard) as the positive basis for the acceptance of authentic reality, or (as with Sartre) as the negative basis for the rejection of a religious view of the world.

1. The absurd is — that the eternal truth has come into being in time, that God has come into being, has been born, has grown up, and so forth, precisely like any other individ-ual human being, quite indistinguishable from other indi-viduals . . . The absurd is precisely by its objective repulsion the measure of the intensity of faith in inwardness . . . The absurd is the object of faith, and the only object that can be believed. — Søren Kierkegaard, *Concluding Unscientific Postscript*, 188.

2. God's passion is to be found in the absurd; where this sign is to be seen, there God is present; it is as though one

2

heard his voice there, in a sense more terrible than in the thunder, for the distance of the absurd is greater. — Kierkegaard, *The Last Years*, 107.

3. Combinations of logically compatible words become absurd when they contradict the meaningful order of reality. Therefore, the absurd lies in the neighborhood of the grotesque consequences. Such absurdities, however, have no relation to the paradox of the Christian message. — Paul Tillich, *Systematic Theology*, II, 91.

4. Jean-Paul Sartre is of the opinion that when we reflect upon the world as it actually exists, we experience the absurd. Existence itself is unreasonable, and man in particular is unnecessary and superfluous.

5. Karl Jaspers rejects the absurd as defined and celebrated by Kierkegaard. Such absurdity is an indication of the bankruptcy of modern Christianity, Protestant and Catholic. The conception of the "subjective thinker" destroys communication. It may awaken, but cannot transmit thought. Philosophy must return from the mystical to the ethical. "The problem for us is to philosophize without being exceptions, but with our eyes on the exception." — Karl Jaspers, *The Philosophy of Karl Jaspers*, 615.

6. Albert Camus began with the declaration that the world was absurd and meaningless. Refusing to be defeated by such a reality, he celebrated the joy of what he called "the invincible summer" within. By choosing to surmount his own fate, by choosing to live by his own terms in a futile world, man can prove to be greater than any adversity.

See also: Nausea.

ACTAEON COMPLEX: (Greek *Aktaion*, the name of the hunter who angered the lovely goddess Artemis by watching her bathe; she punished him by changing him into a stag, and he was then torn to pieces by his own hunting dogs)

3

The term used by Sartre in *Being and Nothingness* to indicate the totality of images which show that knowing is a form of appropriative volition with overtones of sexuality. In other words, knowledge is what one decides is useful to him, and this decision at least in part is sexual.

AESTHETIC: (Greek *aisthetikos*, sensitive, from *aisthanesthai*, to perceive)

Viewing truth with passion, existentialists unite philosophy with literature. Jean-Paul Sartre has written many excellent short stories, plays, and novels. Søren Kierkegaard and Friedrich Nietzsche exhibit the same talent for literature as they do for technical philosophy.

Kierkegaard used "aesthetical" in a technical way in his thought. The aesthetical is the first "stage on life's way," or "sphere of existence." The aesthetical is that sphere of existence in which a person lives rather aimlessly, seeking pleasure. The aesthetical is the lowest mode of human life.

1. Kierkegaard wrote that the aesthetic stage on life's way, characterized by pleasure, was the lowest of three ways of living, the other two being the ethical and the religious. The aesthetic way of living breaks down when it becomes boring. Then the aimless life of pleasure-seeking is exchanged for the moral life of the ethical man, until this too breaks down in preparation for the religious.

2. In the preface I addressed to Richard Wagner I claimed that art, rather than ethics, constituted the essential metaphysical activity of man, while in the body of the book I made several suggestive statements to the effect that existence could be justified only in esthetic terms. As a matter of fact, throughout the book I attributed a purely esthetic meaning — whether implied or overt — to a process; a kind of divinity in your life, God as the supreme artist, amoral, recklessly creating and destroying, realizing himself indifferently in whatever he does or undoes, ridding himself by his acts of the

4

embarrassment of his riches and the strain of his internal contradictions. Thus the world was made to appear, at every instant, as a successful solution of God's own tensions, as an ever new vision projected by that grand sufferer for whom illusion is the only possible mode of redemption. That whole esthetic metaphysics might be rejected out of hand as so much prattle or rant. Yet in its essential traits it already prefigured that spirit of deep distrust and defiance which, later on, was to resist to the bitter end any moral interpretation of existence whatsoever. It is here that one could find — perhaps for the first time in history — a pessimism situated "beyond good and evil"; a "perversity of stance" of the kind Schopenhauer spent all his life fulminating against; a philosophy which dared place ethics among the phenomena (and so "demote" it) — or, rather, place it not even among the phenomena in the idealistic sense but among the "deceptions." Morality, on this view, became a mere fabrication for purposes of gulling. — Friedrich Nietzsche, *The Birth of Tragedy,* 9, 10.

3. Much will have been gained for esthetics once we have succeeded in apprehending directly — rather than merely ascertaining — that art owes its continuous evolution to the Apollonian-Dionysiac duality, even as the propagation of the species depends on the duality of the sexes. — Friedrich Nietzsche, *The Birth of Tragedy,* 19.

4. The fine arts make our visible world speak to us. We see things as art teaches us to see them. We experience space through the form the architect has imposed upon it; we experience a landscape as it has been epitomized in its religious architecture, shaped by human labor, and made a part of life by constant use. We experience nature and man only as they are reduced to their essence in sculpture, drawing and painting. In a sense, it is when this is done, and only when this is done, that things assume their characteristic form and reveal their visible quality and soul which had previously seemed hidden.

We must distinguish between art as expression of a par-

5

ticular aesthetic ideal and art as a code of symbols for metaphysical reality. The two coincide only when beauty happens to reveal transcendent reality, when such reality is experienced as beautiful, and when everything is seen as essentially beautiful for the reason that it is real. The term "great art" we reserve for metaphysical art — that is to say, an art whose visible creations reveal the underlying reality. It is axiomatic that all representation not so self-transcendent — all mere decoration, all performance which merely charms the senses — can never be more than art in the sense of technical cleverness with no relation to philosophy. This holds true wherever the aesthetic has become divorced from metaphysical contexts. — Karl Jaspers, *Tragedy Is Not Enough,* 25, 26.

5. As a concept of aesthetics, too, the tragic has acquired a coloring which corresponds to this misleading type of tragic philosophy, as when Bahnsen speaks of tragedy as the universal law, or Unamuno of the tragic sense of life. — Karl Jaspers, *Tragedy Is Not Enough,* 98.

6. Sartre has a great interest in questions of value in aesthetics. For instance, in his analysis of the mobiles by Calder, he writes:

In short, although Calder has no desire to imitate anything — his one aim is to create chords and cadences of unknown movements — his mobiles are at once lyrical inventions, technical, almost mathematical combinations and the perceptible symbol of Nature: great elusive Nature, squandering pollen and abruptly causing a thousand butterflies to take wing and never revealing whether she is the blind concatenation of causes and effects or the gradual unfolding however retarded, disconcerted and thwarted, of an idea. — Jean-Paul Sartre, *The Philosophy of Existentialism,* 422.

ANGUISH: (Latin *angustia,* tightness or distress, from *angere,* to tighten, choke)

One of the key terms in existential philosophy, anguish (or

6

dread) reveals the character of human life and illuminates the nature of the world.

1. In Kierkegaard's conception, dread (Danish: *Angest*) is not fear, caused by some external threat. Rather, dread is an inward passion, either a continuous melancholy or a sudden and terrifying emotion. "Dread is a sympathetic aversion and an averse sympathy." — Søren Kierkegaard, *Samlede Vaerker*, VI, 136.

2. For Nietzsche a positive valuation was appropriate to the subject of fear:

For fear — that is man's original and fundamental feeling; through fear everything is explained, original sin and original virtue. Through fear there grew also my virtue, that is to say: Science. — Friedrich Nietzsche, *Thus Spake Zarathustra*, 339.

3. Jaspers, differing from Sartre, defines anguish (German: *Angst*) as:

the dizziness and shudder of freedom confronting the necessity of making a choice. — in *The Philosophy of Karl Jaspers*, xvi.

As he develops his thought, anguish is experienced in those ultimate situations, such as before death, in which *Existenz* faces its most extreme limits. In anguish man realizes that he is not strong enough to leap over the abyss which has opened before him, yet, paradoxically, if he leaps into the calm, he will succeed.

4. Heidegger uses the term extensively, as the following selections indicate:

As a state-of-mind which will satisfy these methodological requirements, the phenomenon of *anxiety* will be made basic for our analysis. In working out this basic state-of-mind and characterizing ontologically what is disclosed in it as such, we shall take the phenomenon of falling as our point of departure, and distinguish anxiety from the kindred phenomenon, of fear, which we have analysed earlier. As one of Dasein's possibilities of Being, anxiety — together with Dasein itself as disclosed in it — provides the phenomenal basis for explicitly grasping Dasein's primordial totality of Being. Dasein's Being reveals itself as *care*. — Martin Heidegger, *Being and Time*, 227.

5. How is the temporality of *Anxiety* related to that of fear? We have called the phenomenon of anxiety a basic state-of-mind. Anxiety brings Dasein face to face with its ownmost Being-thrown and reveals the uncanniness of everyday familiar Being-in-the-world. — Martin Heidegger, *Being and Time*, 393.

6. Anxiety discloses an insignificance of the world, and this insignificance reveals the nullity of that with which one can concern oneself — or, in other words, the impossibility of projecting oneself upon a potentiality-for-Being which belongs to existence and which is founded primarily upon one's objects of concern. — Martin Heidegger, *Being and Time*, 393.

7. *The character of have been is constitutive for the state-of-mind of anxiety; and bringing one face to face with repeatability is the specific ecstatical mode of this character.* Martin Heidegger, *Being and Time*, 394.

8. The existential meaning of anxiety is such that it cannot lose itself in something it might be concerned with. — Martin Heidegger, *Being and Time*, 394.

9. Sartre treats anguish (French: *angoises)* as the reflective apprehension of the Self as freedom. Anguish is the realization that a nothingness slips in between my Self and my past and future so that nothing relieves me from the necessity of continually choosing myself and nothing guarantees the validity of the values which I choose. Fear, on the other hand, is fear of something in the world. Anguish is anguish before myself.

Kierkegaard describing anguish in the face of what one lacks characterizes it as anguish in the face of freedom. But Heidegger, whom we know to have been greatly influenced by Kierkegaard, considers anguish instead as the apprehension of nothingness. The two descriptions of anguish do not appear to us contradictory; on the contrary the one implies the other.

First we must acknowledge that Kierkegaard is right; anguish is distinguished from fear in that fear is fear of beings in the world whereas anguish is anguish before myself. Vertigo is anguish to the extent that I am afraid not of falling over the precipice, but of throwing myself over. — Jean-Paul Sartre, *Being and Nothingness,* 29.

10. What do we mean by anguish? The existentialist frankly states that man is in anguish. His meaning is as follows — When a man commits himself to anything, fully realizing that he is not only choosing what he will be, but is thereby at the same time a legislator deciding for the whole of mankind — in such a moment a man cannot escape from the sense of complete and profound responsibility. There are many indeed, who show no such anxiety. But we affirm that they are merely disguising their anguish or are in flight from it. Certainly, many people think that in what they are doing they commit no one but themselves to anything: and if you ask them, "What would happen if everyone did so?" they shrug their shoulders and reply, "Everyone does not do so." but in truth, one ought always to ask oneself what would happen if everyone did as one is doing; nor can one escape from that disturbing thought except by a kind of self-deception. The man who lies in self-excuse, by saying "Everyone will not do it" must be ill at ease in his conscience, for the act of lying implies the universal value which it denies. By its very disguise his anguish reveals itself. This is the anguish that Kierkegaard called "the anguish of Abraham." — Jean-Paul Sartre, *Existentialism Is a Humanism,* 292, 293.

11. It is anguish pure and simple, of the kind well known to all those who have borne responsibilities. When, for instance, a military leader takes upon himself the responsibility for an attack and sends a number of men to their death, he chooses to do it and at bottom he alone chooses. No doubt he acts under a higher command, but its orders, which are more general, require interpretation by him and

upon that interpretation depends the life of ten, fourteen or twenty men. In making the decision, he cannot but feel a certain anguish. All leaders know that anguish. It does not prevent their acting, on the contrary it is the very condition of their action, for the action presupposes that there is a plurality of possibilities, and in choosing one of these, they realize that it has value only because it is chosen. Now it is anguish of that kind which existentialism describes, and moreover, as we shall see, makes explicit through direct responsibility towards other men who are concerned. Far from being a screen which could separate us from action, it is a condition of action itself. — Jean-Paul Sartre, *Existentialism Is a Humanism,* 293, 294.

12. In anguish we do not simply apprehend the fact that the possibles which we project are perpetually eaten away by our freedom-to-come; in addition we apprehend our choice — i.e., ourselves — as unjustifiable. — Jean-Paul Sartre, *Being and Nothingness,* 440.

13. Most of the time we flee anguish in bad faith. — Jean-Paul Sartre, *Being and Nothingness,* 532.

14. Tillich writes that anxiety is a normal factor in existence, and consequently analyzes anxiety in terms of the experiences of fate and death, of emptiness and meaninglessness, and of guilt and condemnation:

I suggest that we distinguish three types of anxiety according to the three directions in which nonbeing threatens being. Nonbeing threatens man's ontic self-affirmation, relatively in terms of fate, absolutely in terms of death. It threatens man's spiritual self-affirmation, relatively in terms of emptiness, absolutely in terms of meaninglessness. It threatens man's moral self-affirmation, relatively in terms of guilt, absolutely in terms of condemnation. . . . In all three forms anxiety is existential in the sense that it belongs to existence as such and not to an abnormal state of mind as in neurotic (and psychotic) anxiety. — Paul Tillich, *The Courage to Be,* 41.

15. The normal, existential anxiety of guilt drives the person toward attempts to avoid this anxiety (usually called the uneasy conscience) by avoiding guilt. Moral self-discipline and habits will produce moral perfection although one remains aware that they cannot remove the imperfection which is implied in man's existential situation, his estrangement from his true being. Neurotic anxiety does the same thing but in a limited, fixed, and unrealistic way. The anxiety of becoming guilty, the horror of feeling condemned, are so strong that they make responsible decisions and any kind of moral action almost impossible. . . . The moralistic self-defense of the neurotic makes him see guilt where there is no guilt or where one is guilty only in a very indirect way. — Paul Tillich, *The Courage to Be*, 75, 76.

B

BAD FAITH: (French *Mauvaise Foi*)

Lying to oneself, in Sartre (q.v.). For example, bad faith is when one pretends that something is inevitable when it is not. Bad faith is pretending that one must behave in such a way when in fact one chooses to behave thus.

Bad faith includes (1) most appeals to duty, (2) saying "you couldn't help what you did," (3) thinking that one *must* return hospitality, (4) thinking that one *must* get up in the morning, or (5) that one must be polite. Bad faith is the attempt to escape from the anguish men suffer when they are brought face to face with their own freedom.

Bad faith is a self-evident fact of existence. It proves the existence of the power to conceive non-existence. The necessary condition of bad faith is the grasping of nothingness which is identical with the freedom of consciousness. Sartre has been criticized for holding that bad faith is self-evident.

BEING: (*Be* is a defective verb with parts from three unrelated stems: (1) Indo-European base **es-*, as in Sanskrit *ásmi, asti*, Gothic *im, ist*, English *am, is;* (2) Indo-European base **wes-*, stay, remain, as in Sanskrit *vasati*, lingers, stays, Gothic *wisan, was, wēsum*, remain, be, English *was, were;* (3) Indo-European base **bheu-*, grow, become, as in Sanskrit *bhávati*, occurs, is there, Latin *fieri* (*fis, fit, fimus*) be, become, occur)

In general philosophical usage, being is that which "is", without qualification. According to Spinoza, being is both the source and the ultimate subject of all distinctions. According to Hegel, being contains non-being within itself and is the source of the cosmic process which leads to the synthetic union of being and non-being in becoming. Tillich uses the term being to mean the whole of human reality, not existence in time and space.

According to Kierkegaard, it is important to note carefully what is meant by being:

1. (Danish: *Vaeren*) If being . . . is understood as empirical being, truth is at once transformed into a *desideratum,* and everything must be understood in terms of becoming; for the empirical object is unfinished and the existing cognitive spirit is itself in process of becoming. Thus the truth becomes an approximation whose beginning cannot be posited absolutely, precisely because the conclusion is lacking, the effect of which is retroactive. . . . The term "being," as used in the above definitions, must therefore be understood (from the systematic standpoint) much more abstractly, presumably as the abstract reflection of, or the abstract prototype for, what being is as concrete empirical being. When so understood there is nothing to prevent us from abstractly determining the truth as abstractly finished and complete; for the correspondence between thought and being is, from the abstract point of view, always finished. Only with the concrete does becoming enter in, and it is from the concrete that abstract thought abstracts. — Søren Kierkegaard (Johannes Climacus), *Concluding Unscientific Postscript to the Philosophical Fragments,* 169, 170.

2. According to Jaspers, being (German: *Sein*) cannot be defined unequivocally. Being generally represents authentic reality. It is the unconditional, infinite, all-encompassing and all-transcending primal source:

Being is not produced by us; it is not mere interpretation. . . Rather, by its own impetus, it causes us to interpret and will not permit our interpretation ever to be satisfied. — Jaspers, in *The Philosophy of Karl Jaspers,* xvii.

14

Jaspers also refers to "being as freedom" and "being as status." By "being as freedom," he means:

The mode of my being as *Existenz*. In this sense I am origin: not the origin of Being as such, but origin for myself in existence (Dasein). — Jaspers, in *The Philosophy of Karl Jaspers*, xvii.

"Being as status" refers to the

Being which must be acknowledged is directly there as a thing. I can grasp it directly, do something with it: technically with the things, argumentatively with myself and with other consciousness. . . . Everywhere it is an objectively given being. — Jaspers, *Ibid.*

3.   Heidegger's characteristic contribution to the study of being is that

Being cannot be grasped except by taking time into considertion. — Heidegger, *Being and Time*, 40.

Time needs to be *explicated primordially as the horizon for the understanding of Being, and in terms of temporality as the Being of Dasein, which understands Being.* — Heidegger, *Being and Time*, 39.

Being, as the basic theme of philosophy, is no class or genus of entities; yet it pertains to every entity. Its "universality" is to be sought higher up. Being and the structure of Being lie beyond every entity and every possible character which an entity may possess. *Being is the transcendens pure and simple.* And the transcendence of Dasein's Being is distinctive in that it implies the possibility and the necessity of the most radical *individuation*. Every disclosure of Being as the *transcendens* is *transcendental* knowledge. — Heidegger, *Being and Time*, 62.

The famous question Heidegger asked, quoted many times by Paul Tillich, was

Why is there something and not nothing? — Heidegger, *Introduction to Metaphysics.*

4.   Sartre, generally following Heidegger's thought, writes

15

that Being (French: *Être*) is equally beyond negation as beyond affirmation. — Sartre, *Being and Nothingness,* lxv.

The first being which we meet in our ontological inquiry is the being of the appearance. . . . Being will be disclosed to us by some kind of immediate access — boredom, nausea, etc., and ontology will be the description of the phenomenon of being as it manifests itself; that is, without intermediary. — Sartre, B*eing and Nothingness,* xlviii.

Being is. Being is in-itself. Being is what it is. These are the three characteristics which the preliminary examination of the phenomenon of being allows us to assign to the being of phenomena. . . . Thus we have left "appearances" and have been led progressively to posit two types of being, the in-itself and the for-itself. — Sartre, *Being and Nothingness,* lxvi, lxvii. Being-in-itself *is.* This means that being can neither be derived from the possible nor reduced to the necessary. . . . Being-in-itself is never either possible or impossible. It *is.* . . . Uncreated, without reason for being, without any connection with another being, being-in-itself is *de trop* for eternity. — Sartre, *Being and Nothingness,* lxvi.

5. According to Berdyaev,

We should help the progression of philosophical theory by admitting that *knowledge is the apprehension of Being through Being,* that the knowing subject is not opposed to Being as to an object, but is an entity in himself. In other words, *the subject is existential.* The existential nature of the subject is one of the spiritual ways of apprehending the mystery of Being; it is an apprehension based not upon the outward opposition of philosophy and Being, but on their inward and intimate union. Thus true knowledge is an illumination of Being— an *Aufklärung,* to restore the real sense of a term which the eighteenth century had degraded and falsified. — Nicolas Berdyaev, *Solitude and Society,* 42.

In the depths of Being there is an obscure irrational substratum with which knowledge cannot be identified, but which it is its task to illuminate. — Nicolas Berdyaev, *Solitude and Society,* 43.

6. Paul Tillich directly relates the question of being to the central concerns of theology:

> Our ultimate concern is that which determines our being or not-being. Only those statements are theological which deal with their object in so far as it can become a matter of being or not-being for us. —Paul Tillich, *Systematic Theology,* I, 14.

> If one is asked how nonbeing is related to being-itself, one can only answer metaphorically: being "embraces" itself and nonbeing. Being has nonbeing "within" itself as that which is eternally present and eternally overcome in the process of the divine life. The ground of everything that is is not a dead entity without movement and becoming; it is living creativity. Creatively it affirms itself, eternally conquering its own nonbeing. As such it is the pattern of the self-affirmation of every finite being and the source of the courage to be. — Tillich, *The Courage to Be,* 34.

C

CONSCIENCE: (Latin *conscientia,* consciousness, feeling, knowledge).

Existentialists are divided in their view of conscience. Some consider conscience to be the moral voice within the individual, helpful and necessary. Others believe conscience to be the product of society and thus completely relative.

1. Kierkegaard believed the conscience to be beneficial:

You and conscience are one. It knows all that you know, and it knows that you know it. — Søren Kierkegaard, *Purity of Heart Is to Will One Thing,* 189.

What is eternity's accounting other than that the voice of conscience is forever instilled with its eternal right to be the exclusive voice? What is it other than that throughout eternity an infinite stillness reigns wherein the conscience may talk with the individual about what he, as an individual, of what he has done of Good or of evil, and about the fact that during his life he did not wish to be an individual? What is it other than that within eternity there is infinite space so that each person, as an individual, is apart with his conscience? For in eternity there is no mob pressure, no crowd, no hiding place in the crowd, as little as there are riots or street fights! Here in the temporal order, in the unrest, in the noise, in the pressure of the mob, in the crowd, in the primeval forest of evasion, alas, it is true, the calamity still happens, that someone completely stifles the voice of his conscience — his conscience, for he can never rid himself of it. It continues to belong to him, or more accurately, he continues to belong to it. Yet we are not now talking about this calamity, for even among the better persons, it happens all too readily that the voice of conscience becomes merely one voice among many. Then it follows so easily that the isolated voice of conscience (as generally happens to a solitary one) becomes overruled — by the majority. But in eternity, conscience is the only voice that is heard. It must be heard by the individual, for the individual has become the eternal echo of this voice. It must be heard. There is no place to flee from it. For in the infinite there is no place, the individual is himself the place. It must be heard. In vain the individual looks about for the crowd. Alas, it is as if there were a world between him and the nearest individual, whose conscience is also speaking to him about what *he* as an individual has spoken, and done, and thought of good and of evil. — Kierkegaard, *Purity of Heart Is to Will One Thing,* 186, 187.

2. Nietzsche believed that the conscience was derived from the pressures of society, the gradual result of centuries of military, legal, educational, and psychological suppression by the ruling groups. Man should only heed the transmoral conscience of the Overman, or superman *(übermensch),* according to Nietzsche.

3. If we train our conscience, it kisses us while it hurts us. — Nietzsche, *Beyond Good and Evil,* 83.

4. To be ashamed of one's immorality — that is a step on the staircase at whose end one is also ashamed of one's morality. — Nietzsche, *Beyond Good and Evil,* 83.

5. ' His proud awareness of the extraordinary privilege responsibility confers has penetrated deeply and become a dominant instinct. What shall he call that dominant instinct, provided he ever feels impelled to give it a name? Surely he will call it his *conscience.*

His conscience? It seems a foregone conclusion that this conscience, which we encounter here in its highest form, has behind it a long history of transformations. — Nietzsche, *The Genealogy of Morals,* 191, 192.

6. There can be no doubt that bad conscience is a sickness, but so, in a sense, is pregnancy. — Nietzsche, *The Genealogy of Morals,* 221.

7. *Conscience discourses solely and constantly in the mode of keeping silent.* — Heidegger, *Being and Time,* 318 (273).

8. Everything obliges us to recognize that fidelity to oneself is both difficult to achieve and to discern. In order to be faithful to oneself it is first of all necessary to remain alive, and that is precisely what is is not so easy to do. The causes within and without us which militate in favour of sclerosis and devitalisation are innumerable. But these words are not perfectly adequate; it would be better to say that I tend to become increasingly profane in relation to a certain mystery of my *self* to which access is more and more strictly forbidden me. I should add that this unquestionably comes about in so far as the child that I used to be, and that I should have remained were I a poet, dies a little more each day. This profane self is a deserter, having adopted the point of view of "the outsiders". For such a self fidelity tends to be reduced to a stubbornly maintained agreement between myself and certain expressions, ideas, ways of living, to which I have fixed the label *mine.* But this agreement is only maintained at the expense of a certain intimacy, now broken and lost.

If, however, we make an honest enquiry, experience will force us to the paradoxical conclusion that the more I am able to preserve this intimacy with myself, the more I shall be capable of making real contact with my neighbour, and by neighbour I do not mean one of those depersonalized others whose jeers and censure I fear, but the particular human being I met at a definite time in my life and who, even though I may never see him again, has come for good into the personal universe which, as it were, wraps me round — my spiritual atmosphere, which, perhaps I shall take with me in death. — Gabriel Marcel, *Homo Viator*, 131.

9. The proposition, "the voice of conscience is the voice of God" is not absolutely valid: for conscience, too, can deceive. — Karl Jaspers, *Myth and Christianity*.

D

DASEIN: The German term customarily left untranslated in Heidegger's philosophical writings. *Dasein* literally means "Being there," or, in other words, being in a particular place. Hence *Dasein* is used to mean human existence.

In traditional German philosophy, *Dasein* was used in a general way to stand for almost any kind of Being or existence which something has, for example, the existence of God. In common usage, *Dasein* was used to stand for the kind of existence which belongs to persons. Thus it can be seen that Heidegger followed the more everyday usage, with the exception that he often uses it to stand for any person who has such Being, and who is thus an 'entity' himself.

> 1. As ways in which man behaves, sciences have the manner of Being which this entity — man himself — possesses. This entity we denote by the term *"Dasein"*. Scientific research is not the only manner of Being which this entity can have, nor is it the one which lies closest. Moreover, Dasein itself has a special distinctiveness as compared with other entities, and it is worth our while to bring this to view in a provisional way. . . . Dasein is an entity which does not just occur among other entities. Rather it is ontically distinguished by the fact that, in its very being, that Being is an *issue* for it. . . . *Understanding of Being is itself a definite characteristic of Dasein's Being.* Dasein is ontically distinctive in that it *is* ontological. — Heidegger, *Being and Time,* 32 (11, 12).

DEATH: (Indo-European base **dheu-,* to become senseless)

One of the preoccupations of existential philosophy, death for Sartre proves the absurdity of life. Existential thinkers on the whole are concerned to define and interpret death properly so that man is encouraged to face death with reckless freedom, embracing its absurdity yet not permitting death to rob life of all meaning and freedom.

1. When death is the greatest danger, one hopes for life; but when one becomes acquainted with an even more dreadful danger, one hopes for death. — Søren Kierkegaard, *The Sickness Unto Death,* 151.

2. We know we shall die. Of being dead we know nothing. What we had clung to as knowledge, or as knowledge determined by faith, is struck from our hands.

Man's task is to live in hazard and danger, throwing the light of the highest criteria on the situations given him. To know of his immortality as a fact would rob him of his being. Holding out against not knowing brings him to himself and sets him on his proper path.

Lessing has said: "Why can't we wait quietly for a future life as though it were a future day? . . . If there were a religion that instructed us beyond all doubt about that life, we would do better to pay it no heed." — Jaspers, *Philosophy Is for Everyman,* 113.

3. The thought of death can give rise to the fear of not living authentically. One glimpse of the void within and without, and we take refuge in ceaseless activity, eschewing reflection. But the secret restlessness remains. The life force delivers us from it only in appearance; only the sheer force of the thought of death itself frees us in truth. It affirms that other than merely vital significance of man: the eternal weight of his love. Peace in the face of death springs from the awareness of what no death can take away. — Jaspers, *Philosophy Is for Everyman,* 113.

4. We die speeding toward the beloved dead. They receive

us into their circle. Not an empty nothingness receives us, but the plenitude of life truly lived. We step into a space filled with love, lit by truth. — Jaspers, *Philosophy Is for Everyman,* 115.

5. When asked: Why death? Alcmaeon, the Pythagorean and physician, who lived in the sixth century before Christ, answered: "Men die because they lack the power to join the beginning to the end." Anyone who can do that is immortal. Jaspers, *Philosophy Is for Everyman,* 108.

6. What does that mean? The circle of time, considered as recurrence, is the immortality of what happens in this circle. This does not happen of itself, but thanks to a "power" of which Alcmaeon spoke. That is what Nietzsche meant: Belief in the Eternal Return is the strangest act of life-affirmation. — Jaspers, *Philosophy Is for Everyman,* 108, 109.

7. MY DEATH: After death had appeared to us as pre-eminently non-human since it was what there was on the other side of the "wall," we decided suddenly to consider it from a wholly different point of view — that is, as an event of human life. This change is easily explained: death is a boundary, and every boundary (whether it be final or initial) is a Janus bifrons. Whether it is thought of as adhering to the nothingness of being which limits the process considered or whether on the contrary it is revealed as adhesive to the series which it terminates, in either case it is a being which belongs to an existent process and which in a certain way constitutes the meaning of the process. Thus the final chord of a melody always looks on the one side toward silence — that is, toward the nothingness of sound which will follow the melody; in one sense it is made with the silence since the silence is already present in the resolved chord as its meaning. But on the other side it adheres to this plenum of being which is the melody intended, without the chord this melody would remain in the air, and this final indecision would flow back from note

25

to note to confer on each of them the quality of being unfinished. — Sartre, *Being and Nothingness*, 507, 508.

8. We may now summarize our characterization of authentic Being-towards-death as we have projected it existentially: *anticipation reveals to Dasein its lostness in the they-self, and brings it face to face with the possibility of being itself, primarily unsupported by concernful solicitude, but of being itself, rather, in an impassioned freedom towards death — a freedom which has been released from the illusions of the "they", and which is factical, certain of itself, and anxious.* — Heidegger, *Being and Time*, 311 (266).

9. Thus we must conclude in opposition to Heidegger that death, far from being my peculiar possibility, is a *contingent fact* which as such on principle escapes me and originally belongs to my facticity. I can neither discover my death nor wait for it nor adopt an attitude toward it, for it is that which is revealed as undiscoverable, that which disarms all waiting, that which slips into all attitudes (and particularly into those which are assumed with respect to death) so as to transform them into externalized and fixed conducts whose meaning is forever entrusted to others and not to ourselves, Death is a pure fact as is birth; it comes to us from outside and it transforms us into the outside. At bottom it is in no way distinguished from birth, and it is the identity of birth and death that we call facticity. — Sartre, *Being and Nothingness*, 521.

10. When Heidegger speaks about the anticipation of one's own death it is not the question of immortality which concerns him but the question of what the anticipation of death means for the human situation. — Tillich, *The Courage to Be*, 142.

11. Passion, i.e. the expression of the highest intensity of life, always holds the menace of death. He who accepts love in its overwhelming power and tragedy, accepts death. He who attaches too much value to life and avoids death, runs away from love and sacrifices it to other tasks of life. In

erotic love the intensity of life reaches its highest pitch and leads to destruction and death. The lover is doomed to death and involves the loved one in his doom. In the second act of *Tristan and Isolde* Wagner gives a musical revelation of this. The herd-mind tries to weaken the connection between love and death, to safeguard love and settle it down in this world. But it is not even capable of noticing love. It organizes the life of the race and knows only one remedy against death — birth. — Berdyaev, *The Destiny of Man*, 254.

12. Death is . . . what it signifies and, moreover, what it signifies to a being who rises to the highest spiritual level to which it is possible for us to attain. It is evident that if I read in the newspaper of the death of Mr. So-and-so, who is for me nothing but a name, this event *is* for me nothing more than the subject of an announcement. But it is quite another thing in the case of a being who has been granted to me as a presence. In this case, everything depends on me, on my inward attitude of maintaining this presence which could be debased into an effigy. — Marcel, *The Philosophy of Existentialism*, 37.

3. I cannot think of my death except as a future event. . . . It becomes more and more clear that the thought of death can only appear to reflection as a pure fiction. . . . For faith, that is, for thought which has overcome the imaginary, *there is no death.* — Marcel, *Philosophical Fragments*, 96, 97.

14. "To love a being," says one of my characters, "is to say you, you in particular, will never die." — Marcel, *Homo Viator*, 147.

15. Death is an event embracing the whole of life. Our existence is full of death and dying. Life is perpetual dying, experiencing the end in everything, a continual judgment passed by eternity upon time. Life is a constant struggle against death and a partial dying of the human body and the human soul. Death within life is due to the impossibility of embracing the fullness of being, either in time or in space.

Time and space are death-dealing, they give rise to disruptions which are a partial experience of death. — Berdyaev, *The Destiny of Man*, 251.

16. *The meaning of death is that there can be no eternity in time and that an endless temporal series would be meaningless.* — Berdyaev, *The Destiny of Man*, 251.

17. Every kind of evil in the last resort means death. Murder, hatred, malice, depravity, envy, vengeance are death and seeds of death. Death is at the bottom of every evil passion. Pride, greed, ambition are deadly in their results. There is no other evil in the world except death and killing. Death is the evil result of sin. A sinless life would be immortal and eternal. Death is a denial of eternity and therein lies its ontological evil, its hostility to existence, its striving to reduce creation to non-being. Death resists God's creation of the world and is a return to the original non-being. — Berdyaev, *The Destiny of Man*, 252.

18. Death is hideous, the acme of hideousness, it is dissolution, the loss of all image and form, the triumph of the lower elements of the material world. But at the same time death is beautiful, it ennobles the least of mortals and raises him to the level of the greatest, it overcomes the ugliness of the mean and the commonplace. There is a moment when the face of the dead is more beautiful and harmonious than it had been in life. Ugly, evil feelings pass away and disappear in the presence of death. — Berdyaev, *The Destiny of Man*, 253.

19. Death, the greatest of evils, is more noble than life in this world. — Berdyaev, *The Destiny of Man*, 253.

20. Heidegger rightly says that the source of death is "anxiety", but that is a source visible from our everyday world. Death is also a manifestation of eternity, and in our sinful world eternity means terror and anguish. — Berdyaev, *The Destiny of Man*, 260.

21. If our sinful temporal world as we know it were endless, this would be an evil nightmare, just like the endless continuation of an individual life. It would be a triumph of the meaningless. — Berdyaev, *The Destiny of Man,* 261.

22. To achieve communion is to have no fear of death, it is to feel that the power of love is stronger than that of death. Those who have achieved communion are not spared the tragic divorce of death, but for them this divorce is only confined to the natural world. Inwardly, in the spiritual world, it proves the path of true life, since death affects only the objective world and, especially, the personality of those who have surrendered themselves to its alien power. — Berdyaev, *Solitude and Society,* 150.

23. The very word "immortality" is inexact and implies a rejection of the mysterious fact of death. The question of the immortality of the soul forms part of a metaphysic that is utterly out of date. Death is the most profound and significant fact of life, raising the least of mortals above the mean commonplaces of life. The fact of death alone gives true depth to the question as to the meaning of life. Life in this world has meaning just because there is death; if there were no death in our world, life would be meaningless. The meaning is bound up with the end. It there were no end, i.e. if life in our world continued forever, there would be no meaning in it. Meaning lies beyond the confines of this limited world, and the discovery of meaning presupposes an end here. It is remarkable that although men rightly regard it as the supreme evil, they are bound to connect with it the final discovery of meaning. Death — the supreme horror and evil — proves to be the only way out of the "bad time" into eternity; immortal and eternal life prove to be only attainable through death. — Berdyaev, *The Destiny of Man,* 249.

24. Death is an essential motivating force which spurs man on to find self-attainment in his existence. "Death . . . belongs quite properly to life." — Viktor Frankl.

25. A man's birth is an uncontrollable event in his life, but the manner of his departure from life, bears a definite relation to his philosophy of life and death. We are mistaken in considering death a purely biologic event. Life is not comprehended truly or lived fully unless the idea of death is grappled with honestly. — Feifel, in *Existential Psychology*, 73.

26. Death is of course the most obvious form of the threat of non-being. Freud grasped this truth on one level in his symbol of the death instinct. Life forces (being) are arrayed at every moment, he held, against the forces of death (non-being), and in every individual life the latter will ultimately triumph. But Freud's concept of the death instinct is an ontological truth and should not be taken as a deteriorated psychological theory. The concept of the death instinct is an excellent example of our earlier point that Freud went beyond technical reason and tried to keep open the tragic dimension of life. — Rollo May, *Existence*, 48.

27. Along with the great conflict between the increased urge to eat and the dread of becoming fat, the contrast between life in the ethereal world and in the world of the earth (which is also the world of being-fat) continues. Ellen does not want to live as the worm lives in the earth, old, ugly, dumb, and dull — in a word, fat. She would rather die as the bird dies who bursts his throat with supreme jubilation, or she would rather wildly consume herself in her own fire. What is new here is that the longing for death flashes up out of the ethereal world itself. — Ludwig Binswanger, "The Case of Ellen West," in *Existence*, 285.

28. Without suffering and death human life cannot be complete. — Frankl, *From Death Camp to Existentialism*, 67.

29. Only by integrating the concept of death into the self does an authentic and genuine existence become pos-

sible. The price for denying death is undefined anxiety, self-alienation. To completely understand himself, man must confront death, become aware of personal death. — Herman Feifel, in *Existential Psychology,* 65.

30. The popular belief in immortality which in the Western world has largely replaced the Christian symbol of resurrection is a mixture of courage and escape. It tries to maintain one's self-affirmation even in the face of one's having to die. But it does this by continuing one's finitude, that is one's having to die, infinitely, so that the actual death never will occur. This, however, is an illusion and, logically speaking, a contradiction in terms. It makes endless what, by definition, must come to an end. The "immortality of the soul" is a poor symbol for the courage to be in the face of one's having to die. — Tillich, *The Courage to Be,* 169.

31. The anxiety about death is met in two ways. The reality of death is excluded from daily life to the highest possible degree. The dead are not allowed to show that they are dead; they are transformed into a mask of the living. The other and more important way of dealing with death is the belief in a continuation of life after death, called the immortality of the soul. This is not a Christian and hardly a Platonic doctrine. Christianity speaks of resurrection and eternal life, Platonism of a participation of the soul in the transtemporal sphere of essences. But the modern idea of immortality means a continuous participation in the productive process — "time and world without end." It is not the eternal rest of the individual in God but his unlimited contribution to the dynamics of the universe that gives him the courage to face death. In this kind of hope God is almost unnecessary. He may be considered the guarantee of immorality, but *if not,* the belief in immortality is not necessarily shaken. — Tillich, *The Courage to Be,* 110.

DESPAIR: (Latin *de-,* + *spes,* without hope).

For existential thinkers, particularly Kierkegaard, despair is one of the most significant human emotions which provides the spur to fruitful thought about the nature of the human condition. Tillich later repeats the same estimate, adding the qualification that the emotion of despair itself is not necessarily experienced by all or even by the majority of people.

1. (Danish *fortvivelse,* despair or desperation) I would call attention once and for all to the fact that in this whole book, as the title indeed says, despair is conceived as the sickness, not as the cure. So dialectical is despair. — Søren Kierkegaard, *The Sickness unto Death,* 143.

2. Despair is the disrelationship in a relation which relates itself to itself. — Kierkegaard, *The Sickness unto Death,* 148.

3. Yet despair is precisely *self-consuming,* but it is an impotent self-consumption which is not able to do what it wills; and this impotence is a new form of self-consuption, in which again, however, the despairer is not able to do what he wills, namely, to consume himself. — Kierkegaard, *The Sickness unto Death,* 151.

4. If there were nothing eternal in a man, he could not despair; but if despair could consume his self, there would still be no despair. — Kierkegaard, *The Sickness unto Death,* 153, 154.

5. And, oh, when the hour-glass has run out, the hourglass of time, when the noise of worldliness is silenced, and the restless or the ineffectual busyness comes to an end, when everything is still about thee as it is in eternity — whether thou wast man or woman, rich or poor, dependent, fortunate or unfortunate, whether thou didst bear the splendor of the crown in a lofty station, or didst bear only the labor and heat of the day in an inconspicuous lot; whether thy name shall be remembered as long as the world stands (and so was remembered as long as the

world stood), or without a name thou didst cohere as nameless with the countless multitude; whether the glory which surrounded thee surpassed all human description, or the judgment passed upon thee was the most severe and dishonoring human judgment can pass — eternity asks of thee and of every individual among these million millions only one question, whether thou hast lived in despair or not, whether thou wast in despair in such a way that thou didst not know thou wast in despair, or in such a way that thou didst hiddenly carry this sickness in thine inward parts as thy gnawing secret, carry it under thy heart as the fruit of a sinful love, or in such a way that thou, a horror to others, didst rave in despair. And if so, if thou hast lived in despair (whether for the rest thou didst win or lose), then for thee all is lost, eternity knows thee not, it never knew thee, or (even more dreadful) it knows thee as thou art known, it puts thee under arrest by thyself in despair. — Kierkegaard, *The Sickness unto Death,* 160, 161.

6. Not to be one's own self is despair. — Kierkegaard, *The Sickness unto Death,* 163.

7. To despair is to lose the eternal. — Kierkegaard, *The Sickness unto Death,* 185.

8. Not only fear and anxiety, but other moods, are founded existentially upon one's having been; this becomes plain if we merely mention such phenomena as satiety, sadness, melancholy, and desperation. — Martin Heidegger, *Being and Time,* 395 (345).

9. The analysis of despair from the point of view of existential analysis can be seen in this extract from the case of Ellen West:

The enslavement to the world which appears in this mode not only brings about quite diverse, dissociated forms of being-oneself, but also causes the world to split into several dissociated worlds. If we want to designate

33

such a mode of existence with one word, none is more fitting than despair, even from the neutral existential-analytic standpoint. This despair again has many subforms which can be more precisely described according to the character of their temporalization and spatialization and their material garb. In our case the temporalization shows the character of a shortening or shrinking of existence, that is, of the sinking of its rich and flexibly articulated ontological structure to a less articulated level: the unity of this structure falls apart into its different ex-stasies; the ontological relation of the ex-stasies to each other dissolves; the ex-stasy "future" recedes more and more, the ex-stasy "past" predominates, and coinciding with this the present becomes the mere Now or, at best, a mere time-span. With respect to spatialization, this modification of the temporalization results in constriction and emptying of the world; with respect to its material consistency, in making into swamp or earth; with respect to its lighting and coloring, it results in gray glooming and black darkening; with respect to its mobility, in congealing and petrification. And all this is — in accord with the indissoluble unity of world and self — only an expression of the modified being-oneself, of the existential narrowness and emptiness, of the existential darkening, and congealing, and being made into swamp. — Ludwig Binswanger, "The Case of Ellen West," in *Existence,* 310.

10. All human life can be interpreted as a continuous attempt to avoid despair. And this attempt is mostly successful. Extreme situations are not reached frequently and perhaps they are never reached by some people. The purpose of an analysis of such a situation is not to record ordinary human experiences but to show extreme possibilities in the light of which the ordinary situations must be understood.— Tillich, *The Courage to Be,* 56.

11. Despair is an ultimate or "boundary-line" situation. One cannot go beyond it. Its nature is indicated in the etymology of the word despair: without hope. No way

out into the future appears. Nonbeing is felt as absolutely victorious. But there is a limit to its victory; nonbeing is *felt* as victorious, and feeling presupposes being. Enough being is left to feel the irresistible power of nonbeing, and this is the despair within the despair. The pain of despair is that a being is aware of itself as unable to affirm itself because of the power of nonbeing. Consequently it wants to surrender this awareness and its presupposition, the being which is aware. It wants to get rid of itself — and it cannot. Despair appears in the form of reduplication, as the desperate attempt to escape despair. If anxiety were only the anxiety of fate and death, voluntary death would be the way out of despair. The courage demanded would be the courage *not* to be. The final form of ontic self-affirmation would be the act of ontic self-negation.

But despair is also the despair about guilt and condemnation. And there is no way of escaping it, even by ontic self-negation. Suicide can liberate one from the anxiety of fate and death — as the Stoics knew. But it cannot liberate from the anxiety of guilt and condemnation, as the Christians know. —Tillich, *The Courage to Be,* 54, 55.

12. — There is only one possible answer, if one does not try to escape the question: namely that the acceptance of despair is in itself faith and on the boundary line of the courage to be. In this situation the meaning of life is reduced to despair about the meaning of life. But as long as this despair is an act of life it is positive in its negativity. Cynically speaking, one could say that it is true to life to be cynical about it. Religiously speaking, one would say that one accepts oneself as accepted in spite of one's despair about the meaning of this acceptance. Tillich, *The Courage to Be,* 175, 176.

E

ENCOMPASSING: (German, *das Umgreifende*)

Karl Jaspers' *(q.v.)* term for the ground underlying the distinction between subject and object. The Encompassing is reminiscent of pre-socratic philosophy, as Anaximander, the Milesian philosopher who flourished in the sixth century B.C., used a similar concept, the *apeiron* (the unlimited, the infinite, in quality) to describe the unity behind the multiplicity of phenomena. Jaspers describes the Encompassing as:

1. What is neither object nor act-of-thinking (subject), but contains both within itself. — Jaspers, *Autobiography,* in *The Philosophy of Karl Jaspers,* xviii.

2. That within which every particular horizon is enclosed as in something absolutely comprehensive which is no longer visible as a horizon at all. — Jaspers, *Reason,* in *The Philosophy of Karl Jaspers,* xviii.

3. Either the *Being in itself* that surrounds us or the *Being that we are.* — Jaspers, *Scope,* in *The Philosophy of Karl Jaspers,* xviii.

4. The Encompassing appears and disappears for us in two opposed perspectives: either as Being itself, in and through which we are — or else as the Encompassing which we ourselves are, and in which every mode of Being appears to us. The latter would be as the medium or condition under which all Being appears as Being for us. — Jaspers, *Reason and Existenz,* 52.

EXISTENCE: (Latin *existere,* to stand forth)

Similar to the scholastic conception, which differentiated being in its actuality from its essence, existential thinkers write of existence as it is in its factuality as opposed to idealistic philosophy (such as hegelianism) which equated essence with existence to the detriment of existence. Passion and responsibility are two of the most significant aspects of existence as viewed by Kierkegaard and Sartre.

1. Existence . . . is used with different meanings. It can mean the possibility of finding a thing within the whole of being, it can mean the actuality of what is potential in the realm of essences, it can mean the "fallen world," and it can mean a type of thinking which is aware of its existential conditions or which rejects essence entirely. Again, an unavoidable ambiguity justifies the use of this one word in these different senses. Whatever exists, that is, "stands out" of mere potentiality, is more than it is in the state of mere potentiality and less than it could be in the power of its essential nature. In some philosophers, notably Plato, the negative judgment on existence prevails. The good is identical with the essential, and existence does not add anything. In other philosophers, notably Ockham, the positive judgment prevails. All reality exists, and the essential is nothing more than the reflex of existence in the human mind. The good is the self-expression of the highest existent — God — and it is imposed on the other existents from outside them. In a third group of philosophers, notably Aristotle, a mediating attitude prevails. The actual is the real, but the essential provides its power of being, and in the highest essence potentiality and actuality are one. — Paul Tillich, *Systematic Theology,* I, 203.

2. (Danish *eksistens)* Existence itself is superior to any demonstration for existence, and hence it is in the given case stupid to ask for proof. Conversely, the inference from essence to existence is a leap. — Søren Kierkegaard, *Concluding Unscientific Postscript,* 38n.

3. Existence itself, the act of existing, is a striving, and is both pathetic and comic in the same degree. It is pathetic because the striving is infinite; that is, it is directed toward the infinite, being an actualization of infinitude, a transformation which involves the highest paths. It is comic, because such a striving involves a self-contradiction. — Kierkegaard, *Concluding Unscientific Postscript*, 84.

4. The thinker who can forget in all his thinking also to think that he is an existing individual, will never explain life. He merely makes an attempt to cease to be a human being, in order to become a book or an objective something. . . . But it will scarcely be pleasant for him to learn that existence itself mocks everyone who is engaged in becoming purely objective. — Kierkegaard, *Concluding Unscientific Postscript*, 85.

5. An existential system is impossible. An existential system cannot be formulated. Does this mean that no such system exists? By no means; nor is this implied in our assertion. Reality itself is a system — for God; but it cannot be a system for any existing spirit. System and finality correspond to one another, but existence is precisely the opposite of finality. — Kierkegaard, *Concluding Unscientific Postscript*, 107.

6. The systematic Idea is the identity of subject and object, the unity of thought and being. Existence, on the other hand, is their separation. It does not by any means follow that existence is thoughtless; but it has brought about, and brings about, a separation between subject and object, thought and being. — Kierkegaard, *Concluding Unscientific Postscript*, 112.

7. It is impossible to exist without passion, unless we understand the word "exist" in the loose sense of a so-called existence. — Kierkegaard, *Concluding Unscientific Postscript*, 276.

8. Existence constitutes the highest interest of the ex-

isting individual, and his interest in his existence constitutes his reality. What reality is cannot be expressed in the language of abstraction.— Kierkegaard, *Concluding Unscientific Postscript,* 279.

9. Nietzsche's justification of the fact of existence is as an "aesthetic phenomenon." In *The Birth of Tragedy* he writes that true culture is the unity of the forces of life, represented by the Dionysian element, with the love of form and beauty, represented by the Apollonian element. The highest product of this true culture will be the creative genius who will then transmute existence into the proper fusion of Dionysian and Apollonian, of life and beauty.

10. Jaspers writes that *Existenz* cannot be defined but only circumscribed. In German philosophy the term *Existenz* had first been used by Hamann and Jacobi in their attack against the rationalism of the Enlightenment and against Kantian Idealism. Later, as Ranke and Schelling opposed Hegel, *Existenz* was used to oppose the concepts of Reason and the Idea.

Jaspers' use of the term *Existenz* explicitly derives from Kierkegaard:

> The word is, to begin with, only one of those which denote being. . . . In philosophy there was from the dark beginnings of history only a presentiment of that which later, through Kierkegaard, gave the word its historically binding meaning for us. — Jaspers, *Philosophie,* in *The Philosophy of Karl Jaspers,* 100.

According to Jaspers' interpretation, Kierkegaard took over from Schelling the distinction between Idea and *Existenz,* thus lifting the existing individual out from every determination by the Hegelian Idea, and thus viewing the existing individual as face to face with an equally indeterminate and indeterminable Godhead.

The word "Existenz" through Kierkegaard has taken on a sense through which we look into infinite depths at what defies all determinate knowledge. The word is not to be taken in its worn-out sense as one of the many synonyms

40

for "being"; it either means nothing, or is to be taken with its Kierkegaardian claims. — Jaspers, *Reason and Existenz*, 49.

11. Jaspers develops a set of existential categories which are analogous to Heidegger's *Existentiale.* The existential categories are directly related to the Kantian categories, being designed to stand over against them.

(a) Existential reality is determined by the central categories of historicity and freedom, as opposed to objective reality which is determined by the laws of causality.

(b) Existential communication corresponds to the causality of substances.

(c) The rank, value, or depth of *Existenz* corresponds to objectively determinable size or greatness.

(d) The fulfilled time of the moment corresponds to endless mathematical time.

12. Jaspers distinguishes four modes of the *Being that we are:* (i) existence, or *Dasein,* (ii) Consciousness-as-such, or *Bewusstein überhaupt,* (iii) spirit, or *Geist,* and (iv) *Existenz.* What he means by these distinctions is explained as follows:

(i) Existence, *Dasein,* denotes the concrete, physio-psychological individual. As the term applies to man, it represents the finding of itself on the part of Being . . . expressed (in such sayings) as: 'I am here,' 'we are here.' — Jaspers, in *The Philosophy of Karl Jaspers*, xix.

(ii) Consciousness-as-such means
the comprehensive consciousness in which everything that is can be known, recognized, intended as an object. — Jaspers, in *The Philosophy of Karl Jaspers*, xviii.

(iii) Spirit represents
the Encompassing which we are as beings who, in the movement of understanding and being understood, realize totality. — Jaspers, in *The Philosophy of Karl Jaspers*, xxii.

(iv) *Existenz*
is what never becomes object, the origin from which issues

41

my thinking and acting. — Jaspers, *Philosophie,* in *The Philosophy of Karl Jaspers,* xix.

Existenz is being a self suspended between itself and Transcendence from which it derives its being and on which it is based. — Jaspers, *Existenz,* in *The Philosophy of Karl Jaspers,* xix.

Being-a-self is called *Existenz.* As such I can become in no manner the object of my own speculation, I cannot know myself, but have only the alternative of either reaching self-realization, or else of losing myself. . . . (Existence is) the axis around which all I am, and all that can become truly meaningful for me in the world turns. — Jaspers, *Wahrheit,* in *The Philosophy of Karl Jaspers,* 99.

13. Being is always the Being of an entity. — Martin Heidegger, *Being and Time,* 29 (9).

14. That kind of Being towards which Dasein can comport itself in one way or another, and always does comport itself somehow, we call *"existence" (Existenz).* And because we cannot define Dasein's essence by citing a "what" of the kind that pertains to a subject-matter, and because its essence lies rather in the fact that in each case it has its Being to be, and has it as its own, we have chosen to designate this entity as "Dasein," a term which is purely an expression of its Being.

Dasein always understands itself in terms of its existence — in terms of a possibility of itself: to be itself or not itself. Dasein has either chosen these possibilities itself, or got itself into them, or grown up in them already. Only the particular Dasein decides its existence, whether it does so by taking hold or by neglecting. The question of existence never gets straightened out except through existing itself. The understanding of oneself which leads *along this way* we call *"existentiell."* The question of existence is one of Dasein's ontical 'affairs.' This does not require that the ontological structure of existence should be theoretically transparent. The question about that structure aims at the analysis of what constitutes existence. The context of such

42

structures we call "existentiality." Its analytic has the character of an understanding which is not existentiell, but rather *existential.* The task of an existential analytic of Dasein has been delineated in advance, as regards both its possibility and its necessity, in Dasein's ontical constitution. — Heidegger, *Being and Time,* 33 (12, 13).

15. The being that exists is man. Man alone exists. Rocks are, but they do not exist. Trees are, but they do not exist. Horses are, but they do not exist. Angels are, but they do not exist. God is, but he does not exist. The proposition "man alone exists" does not mean by any means that man alone is a real being while all other beings are unreal and mere appearances or human ideas. The proposition "man exists" means: man is that being whose Being is distinguished by the open-standing standing-in in the unconcealedness of Being, from Being, in Being. The existential nature of man is the reason why man can represent beings as such, and why he can be conscious of them. All consciousness presupposes ecstatically understood existence as the *essentia* of man — *essentia* meaning that as which man is present insofar as he is man. — Heidegger, *The Way Back into the Ground of Metaphysics,* in *Existentialism from Dostoevsky to Sartre,* 214.

16. To be a self is admittedly one feature of the nature of that being which exists; but existence does not consist in being a self, nor can it be defined in such terms. We are faced with the fact that metaphysical thinking understands man's selfhood in terms of substance or — and at bottom this amounts to the same — in terms of the subject. It is for this reason that the first way which leads away from metaphysics to the ecstatic existential nature of man must lead through the metaphysical conception of human self-hood. — Heidegger, *Ibid.,* 215.

17. The question concerning existence, however, is always subservient to that question which is nothing less than the only question of thought. This question, yet to be unfolded,

concerns the truth of Being as the concealed ground of all metaphysics. — Heidegger, *Ibid.*, 215.

18. Sartre gives both a philosophical and a literary expression to his own conception of the character of existence:

(1) What do we mean by saying that existence precedes essence? We mean that man first of all exists, encounters himself, surges up in the world — and defines afterwards. — Jean-Paul Sartre, *Existentialism,* in *Existentialism from Dostoevsky to Sartre,* 290.

(2) After all, you have to kill time. They are young and well built, they have enough to last them another thirty years. So they're in no hurry, they delay and they are not wrong. Once they have slept together they will have to find something else to veil the enormous absurdity of their existence. — Sartre, *Nausea,* 150.

(3) "I was just thinking," I tell him, laughing, "that here we sit, all of us, eating and drinking to preserve our precious existence and really there is nothing, nothing, absolutely no reason for existing," — Sartre, *Nausea,* 151.

(4) I would so like to let myself go, forget myself, sleep. But I can't, I'm suffocating: existence penetrates me everywhere, through the eyes, the nose, the mouth. — Sartre, *Nausea,* 170.

(5) Even when I looked at things, I was miles from dreaming that they existed: they looked like scenery to me. I picked them up in my hands, they served me as tools, I foresaw their resistance. But that all happened on the surface. If anyone had asked me what existence was, I would have answered, in good faith, that it was nothing, simply an empty form which was added to external things without changing anything in their nature. And then all of a sudden, there it was, clear as day: existence had suddenly unveiled itself. It had lost the harmless look of an abstract category: it was

44

the very paste of things, this root was kneaded into existence. Or rather the root, the park gates, the bench, the sparse grass, all that had vanished: the diversity of things, their individuality, were only an appearance, a veneer. This veneer had melted, leaving soft, monstrous masses, all in disorder — naked, in a frightful, obscene nakedness. — Sartre, *Nausea,* 171, 172.

(6) Existence is not something which lets itself be thought of from a distance: it must invade you suddenly, master you, weigh heavily on your heart like a great motionless beast — or else there is nothing more at all. — Sartre, *Nausea,* 177.

(7) I lost the whole game. At the same time, I learned that you always lose. Only the rascals think they win. Now I am going to be like Anny, I am going to outlive myself. Eat, sleep, sleep, eat. Exist slowly, softly, like these trees, like a puddle of water, like the red bench in the streetcar. — Sartre, *Nausea,* 210.

(8) I know very well that I don't want to do anything: to do something is to create existence — and there's quite enough existence as it is. — Sartre, *Nausea,* 231.

19. Passing from the universality of reason to individual experience is one of the most difficult and perilous tasks. — Gabriel Marcel, *Philosophical Fragments,* 39.

20. Existence cannot be separated from wonder. — Marcel, *Du refus à l'Invocation.*

21. The analysis of existence, including the development of the question implicit in existence, is a philosophical task, even if it is performed by a theologian. — Paul Tillich, *Systematic Theology,* I, 63.

EXISTENTIALISM: The doctrine that existence must be sharply distinguished from essence. The negative aspect of this distinction, that existence cannot be reduced to nor derived from essence, is a universal feature of existentialism properly so called. The positive aspect of this distinction, however, the character and content of authentic existence, may vary considerably from the Christianity of Kierkegaard to the atheistic humanism of Sartre.

Historically, existentialism represents a revolt against traditional philosophy. It denies that truth can ever be synonymous with reason, a central theme in the thought of Plato, Kant, and Hegel. Against the view that existence does not add anything to our conceptual knowledge, existentialism conducts a general examination of existence, its facticity, its emotions, asserting that existence must be the primary category through which such concepts as essence must be viewed.

Existentialism has exerted a profound unifying influence on its analysis of such emotions as anxiety and despair *(q.v.)*. The notion that life is absurd is technically true considered from the point of view of pure reason. That it is emotionally disturbing is one of the key features of Sartre's form of existentialism. None of the pessimistic estimates of the world is taken as grounds for excusing the individual from his responsibility to act and live authentically. Rather, these views are taken as ensuring the more responsible use of the individual's own freedom *(q.v.)*. Existentialists commonly emphasize human freedom and creative choice in the light of a pronounced subjectivity, because of their doctrine that the fact of human existence is prior to any so-called "human nature" or rational scheme of reality.

Existentialism has exerted a profound unifying influence on the usually diverse disciplines of philosophy, theology, literature, and psychology.

The immediate foundations of existentialism were laid by Sǿren Kierkegaard (1813-1855), Friedrich Nietzsche (1844-1900), and to some extent by the phenomenologist Edmund Husserl (1859-1938). The major formulations of existentialism are by Karl Jaspers (1883-1969), Martin Heidegger (1889-   ), and Jean-Paul Sartre (1905-   ). In addition to these thinkers, the most commonly acknowledged philosophical existentialists are Gabriel Marcel (1889-   ), Maurice Merleau-Ponty (1907-1961),

Miguel de Unamuno y Jugo (1864-1936), and Nikolai Aleksandrovich Berdyaev (1874-1948).

The literary existentialists, in addition to many of the above, are Fyodor Mikhailovich Dostoevsky (1821-1881), Rainer Maria Rilke (1875-1926), Franz Kafka (1883-1924), Albert Camus (1913-1960), André Gide (1869-1951), André Malraux (1895-   ).

The most noted men in the field of existential psychology, in addition to Kierkegaard, Jaspers, and Sartre, are Viktor Frankl, Rollo May, Ludwig Binswanger, and Roland Kuhn.

The theological existentialists, in addition to Kierkegaard, Jaspers, and Marcel, are Martin Buber, Karl Barth, Rudolph Bultmann, and Paul Tillich.

Elements of existentialism may be found in earlier thinkers, such as Socrates, the Hebrew Psalmists, Job, St. Paul, St. Augustine, and Pascal, but this is not sufficient justification for calling such thinkers existentialists. Existentialism as a historical philosophical development was a specific reaction against the hegelian form of idealism. Therefore no existentialist in the accurate sense of the term can be found prior to Hegel (1770-1831).

1. The difficulty that inheres in existence, with which the existing individual is confronted, is one that never really comes to expression in the language of abstract thought, much less receives an explanation. Because abstract thought is *sub specie aeterni* it ignores the concrete and the temporal, the existential process, the predicament of the existing individual arising from his being a synthesis of the temporal and the eternal situated in existence. Now if we assume that abstract thought is the highest manifestation of human activity, it follows that philosophy and the philosophers proudly desert existence, leaving the rest of us to face the worst. And something else, too, follows for the abstract thinker himself, namely, that since he is an existing individual he must in one way or another be suffering from absent-mindedness. — Søren Kierkegaard, *Concluding Unscientific Postscript,* 267.

2. By existentialism we mean a doctrine which makes

human life possible and, in addition, declares that every truth and every action implies a human setting and a human subjectivity. — Jean-Paul Sartre, *Existentialism,* in *Existentialism from Dostoevsky to Sartre,* 288.

3. The doctrine that "existence precedes essence, or, if you prefer, that subjectivity must be the starting point." — Sartre, *ibid.,* 289.

4. What complicates matters is that there are two kinds of existentialist; first, those who are Christian, among whom I would include Jaspers and Gabriel Marcel, both Catholic; and on the other hand the atheistic existentialists, among whom I class Heidegger, and then the French existentialists and myself. — Sartre, *ibid.,* 289.

5. Existentialism is nothing else than an attempt to draw all the consequences of a coherent atheistic position. It isn't trying to plunge man into despair at all. . . . Existentialism isn't so atheistic that it wears itself out showing that God doesn't exist. Rather, it declares that even if God did exist, that would change nothing. There you've got our point of view. Not that we believe that God exists, but we think existentialism is optimistic, a doctrine of action. — Sartre, *ibid,* 310.

6. Existentialism stands today at a parting of the ways: it is, in the last analysis, obliged either to deny or to transcend itself. It denies itself quite simply when it falls to the level of infra-dialectical materialism. It transcends itself, or it tends to transcend itself, when it opens itself out to the experience of the suprahuman, an experience which can hardly be ours in a genuine and lasting way this side of death, but of which the reality is attested by mystics. — Gabriel Marcel, *The Philosophy of Existence.*

7. According to Jean Wahl, the term existentialism should be restricted to those philosophers who willingly accept it, specifically:
The Philosophical School of Paris, i.e., Sartre, Simone de

Beauvoir, Marleau-Ponty . . . (for) in our own times Heidegger has opposed what he terms 'Existentialism,' and Jaspers has asserted that 'Existentialism' is the death of the philosophy of existence. — Jean Wahl, *A Short History of Existentialism.*

The difficulty with this view is, first, that even Sartre writes of going beyond existentialism, and, second that criticism of 'Existentialism' as a system of rigidly formalized thought by the German thinkers does not necessarily imply rejection of the key insights of existential philosophy.

8. Existentialism will appear therefore as a fragment of the system, which has fallen outside of Knowledge. From the day that Marxist thought will have taken on the human dimension (that is, the existential project) as the foundation of anthropological Knowledge, existentialism will no longer have any reason for being. Absorbed, surpassed and conserved by the totalizing movement of philosophy, it will cease to be a particular inquiry and will become the foundation of all inquiry. The comments which we have made in the course of the present essay are directed — to the modest limit of our capabilities — toward hastening the moment of that dissolution. — Sartre, *Search for a Method,* 181.

9. Despite a certain affinity between Kierkegaard's philosophy and that of Heidegger and Jaspers, there is yet an essential difference between them. For Kierkegaard, philosophy is itself existence rather than an *interpretation* of existence; whereas, for Heidegger and Jaspers, who are concerned with a particular philosophical tradition, philosophy is synonymous with interpretation. — Nicolas Berdyaev, *Solitude and Society,* 40.

10. Kierkegaard laid the foundations of Existential philosophy by challenging the Hegelian universal concept and its fatal effect on the individual. Kierkegaard's thought is not fundamentally new; it is very simple, and is motivated by the sense of anguish to which the personal drama of his life gave rise. His tragic experience led him to emphasize the

existential character of the knowing subject, the initial fact of man's immersion in the mystery of existence. The philosophy most expressive of man's existential character is the most vital; for philosophers have too often tended to overlook the fact of their own existence as distinct from their power of intellection, and the fact that their philosophy is little more than the translation of their existence. We may therefore conclude, though not in Kierkegaard's own terms, that, from the existential stand-point, the philosopher is situated on the extra-natural plane, that is, in the inmost depth of Being; for the subject is himself a part of Being and, as such, communes with its mystery. . . . In my book *The Philosophy of Freedom,* written some twenty years ago, I had already defined Existential philosophy, though I did not use that term, as a philosophy which *represents* something in itself, which is a manifestation of Being, of existence, as opposed to the type of philosophy which treats of something extraneous, of the objective world. — Berdyaev, *Solitude and Society,* 36, 37.

11. There are Existentialists of a less radical point of view. Karl Jaspers recommends a new conformity in terms of an all-embracing "philosophical faith"; others speak of a *philosophia perennis;* while Gabriel Marcel moves from an Existentialist radicalism to a position based on the semi-collectivism of medieval thought. — Paul Tillich, *The Courage to Be,* 150.

12. Existentialism tries to save the freedom of the individual self from the domination of controlling knowledge. But this freedom is described in terms which not only lack any criterion but also any content. Existentialism is the most desperate attempt to escape the power of controlling knowledge and of the objectified world which technical reason has produced. It says "No" to this world, but, in order to say "Yes" to something else, it has either to use controlling knowledge or to turn to revelation. Tillich, *Systematic Theology,* I, 100.

13. The revolt against Hegel's Essentialist philosophy was accomplished with the help of Existentialist elements present, though subdued, in Hegel himself. The first to lead the Existentialist attack was Hegel's former friend Schelling, on whom Hegel had been dependent in earlier years. In his old age Schelling presented his so-called "Positive Philosophie," most of the concepts of which were used by the revolutionary Existentialists of the 19th century. He called Essentialism "negative philosophy" because it abstracts from real existence, and he called Positive Philosophie the thought of the individual who experiences and thinks, and decides within his historical situation. He was the first to use the term "existence" in contradicting philosophical Essentialism. Although his philosophy was rejected because of the Christian myth which he reinterpreted philosophically in Existentialist terms, he influenced many people, notably Søren Kierkegaard. . . . Marx belonged to the Existential-system of early capitalism with Hegel's Essentialist description of man's reconciliation with himself in the present world. Most important of all the Existentialists was Nietzsche, who in his description of European nihilism presented the picture of a world in which human existence has fallen into utter meaninglessness. . . .

When with July 31, 1914, the 19th century came to an end, the Existentialist revolt ceased to be revolt. It became the mirror of an experienced reality.

It was the threat of an infinite loss, namely the loss of their individual persons, which drove the revolutionary Existentialists of the 19th century to their attack. They realized that a process was going on in which people were transformed into things, into pieces of reality which pure science can calculate and technical science can control. The idealistic wing of bourgeois thinking made of the person a vessel in which universals find a more or less adequate place. The naturalistic wing of bourgeois thinking made of the person an empty field into which sense impressions enter and prevail according to the degree of their intensity. In both cases the individual self is an empty space and the bearer of something which is not himself, something strange by which the self is estranged from itself. Idealism and naturalism are alike in their attitude to the existing person; both of them eliminate his infinite significance and make him a space through which something else passes. — Tillich, *The Courage to Be,* 135-138.

14. The Existentialist protest against dehumanization and objectivation, together with its courage to be as oneself, have turned into the most elaborate and oppressive forms of collectivism that have appeared in history. — Tillich, *The Courage to Be,* 152, 153.

15. One must ask: What is this self that affirms itself? Radical Existentialism answers: What it makes of itself. This is all it can say, because anything more would restrict the absolute freedom of the self. The self, cut off from participation in its world, is an empty shell, a mere possibility. It must act because it lives, but it must redo every action because acting involves him who acts in that upon which he acts. It gives content and for this reason it restricts his freedom to make of himself what he wants. In classical theology, both Catholic and Protestant, only God has this prerogative: He is *ā sē* (from himself) or absolute freedom. Nothing is in him which is not by him. Existentialism, on the basis of the message that God is dead, gives man the divine "a-se-ity." Nothing shall be in man which is not by man. But man is finite, he is given to himself as what he is. He has received his being and with it the structure of his being, including the structure of finite freedom. And finite freedom is not aseity. Man can affirm himself only if he affirms not an empty shell, a mere possibility, but the structure of being in which he finds himself before action and nonaction. Finite freedom has a definite structure, and if the self tries to trespass on this structure it ends in the loss of itself. The nonparticipating hero in Sartre's *The Age of Reason* is caught in a net of contingencies, coming partly from the subconscious levels of his own self, partly from the environment from which he cannot withdraw. The assuredly empty self is filled with contents which enslave it just because it does not know or accept them as contents. This is true too of the cynic, as was said before.

He cannot escape the forces of his self which may drive him into complete loss of the freedom that he wants to preserve. — Paul Tillich, *The Courage to Be,* 151, 152.

16. The last two chapters, that on the courage to be as a part and that on the courage to be as oneself, have shown that the former, if carried through radically, leads to the loss of the self in collectivism and the latter to the loss of the world in Existentialism. — Tillich, *The Courage to Be,* 153, 154.

EXISTENTIAL VACUUM: The psychological condition in which a person doubts that life has any meaning. This new neurosis is characterized by loss of interest and lack of initiative. According to Viktor Frankl, the existential vacuum is apparently a concomitant of industrialization. When neither instinct nor social tradition direct man toward what he ought to do, soon he will not even know what he wants to do, and the existential vacuum results.

1. Not a few cases of suicide could be traced back to this existential vacuum, this lack of a goal. — Viktor Frankl, *From Death Camp to Existentialism.* 100.

2. Because of social pressure, individualism is rejected by most people in favor of conformity. Thus the individual relies mainly upon the actions of others and neglects the meaning of his own personal life. Hence he seen his own life as meaningless and falls into the "existential vacuum" feeling inner void. Progressive automation causes increasing alcoholism, juvenile delinquency, and suicide. — Frankl.

3. Existential frustration makes itself noticeable also in the increasing mass of patients who are turning to the psychiatrist, but who do not come to him with psychic symptoms as with human problems. Some of the people who nowadays call on a psychiatrist would have seen a priest in former days, but now they often refuse to be handed over to a priest, so the doctor is forced into what I once ventured to call

"medical ministry." In our time, also, care of souls has been secularized. Kierkegaard has said: "Preachers are no longer pastors of the souls, but doctors have become such." — Frankl, *From Death Camp to Existentialism,* 106.

F

FREEDOM: (Anglo-Saxon *freo,* not in bondage, noble, glad, illustrious; free, "dear (akin) to the chief", hence "not enslaved.")

Man is essentially free and not determined by any external factor whatever, according to existential thought. Jean-Paul Sartre has formulated the most radical doctrine of freedom in the history of western thought. Accordingly, no limit to human freedom is admitted, neither temporal nor divine. Nothing fetters freedom. The responsibility of an individual for his own deeds, thoughts, and situations is absolute.

1. (Danish *Frihed*) How absurd men are! They never use the liberties they have, they demand those they do not have. They have freedom of thought, they demand freedom of speech. — Søren Kierkegaard (Victor Eremita), *Either/ Or,* 19.

2. In fables and stories of adventure there is mention made of a lamp, called the wonderful; when it is rubbed, a spirit appears. Jest! But freedom is the true wonderful lamp; when a man rubs it with ethical passion, God comes into being for him. And behold, the spirit of the lamp is a servant; so wish for it then, all ye whose spirit is a wish! But whoever rubs the wonderful lamp of freedom becomes himself a servant — the Spirit is Lord. This is the beginning. — Kierkegaard (Johannes Climacus), *Concluding Unscientific Postscript,* 124.

55

3. "Here the vision is free, the spirit exalted." But there is an opposite type of man that is also on a height and also has free vision — but looks *down*. — Friedrich Nietzsche, *Beyond Good and Evil,* 227.

4. Karl Jaspers writes that freedom and *Existenz* are interchangeable concepts. The necessary conditions for freedom are knowledge, arbitrary willing, and law.

(1) Only on the basis of the possibility of my own freedom can I raise the question as to what freedom is. Thus freedom exists either not at all, or else it is already presupposed in the very question concerning it. — Jaspers, in *The Philosophy of Karl Jaspers,* 100.

(2) Freedom wills itself, because it already possesses a grasp of its possibility. — Jaspers, *ibid.,* 100, 101.

(3) Knowledge brings freedom. Outer freedom, which leads knowledge in limited areas to mastery of natural forces, is not spiritually decisive. It is rather inner freedom which is decisive. This freedom is to be seen even in the fact that when I see through something I cease to be merely dependent on some foreign factor. But this freedom is completed only in loving unity with reality. This is the goal of knowledge. — Jaspers, *The European Spirit,* 43, 44.

(4) The will to history grows out of freedom. For the European wishes concrete freedom, that is, the freedom of men in harmony with one another and with the world which fills them.

Only in the West is freedom bound up in the individual consciousness with freedom of circumstances. But since freedom is never attained for everyone and thus in the Western sense is attained for none, history is necessary in order that freedom may be fought for; or the impulse to freedom gives rise to history. — Jaspers, *The European Spirit,* 39.

(5) True freedom does not exist save where it is threatened. — Jaspers.

5. Martin Heidegger, in *Being and Time,* discusses in detail the concept of freedom under the various headings of: freedom for authenticity or inauthenticity, freedom for Being-guilty, freedom for the call of conscience, freedom for care, freedom for death, freedom for freedom of choice, freedom for oneself, freedom for possibilities, freedom for one's ownmost potentiality-for-Being, and freedom for repetition.

(1)   Freedom, however, *is* only in the choice of one possibility — that is, in tolerating one's not having chosen the others and one's not being able to choose them. — Heidegger, *Being and Time,* 331 (285).

(2)   Anxiety makes manifest in Dasein its *Being towards* its ownmost potentiality-for-Being — that is, its *Being-free for* the freedom of choosing itself and taking hold of itself. Anxiety brings Dasein face to face with its *Being-free for* (*propensio in . . .*) the authenticity of its Being, and for this authenticity as a possibility which it always is. — Heidegger, *Being and Time,* 232 (188).

(3)   In so choosing, Dasein makes possible its ownmost Being-guilty, which remains closed off from the they-self. The common sense of the "they" knows only the satisfying of manipulable rules and public norms and the failure to satisfy them. It reckons up infractions of them and tries to balance them off. It has slunk away from its ownmost Being-guilty so as to be able to talk more loudly making "mistakes". But in the appeal, the they-self gets called to the ownmost Being-guilty of the Self. Understanding the call is choosing; but it is not a choosing of conscience, which as such cannot be chosen. What is chosen is *having*-a-conscience as Being-free for one's ownmost Being-guilty, *"Understanding the appeal"* means *"wanting to have a conscience."*

This does not mean that one wants to have a 'good conscience,' still less one cultivates the call voluntarily; it means solely that one is ready to be appealed to. Wanting to have a conscience is just as far from seeking one's factical indebtedness as it is from the tendency to *liberation* from guilt in the sense of the essential 'guilty.'

Wanting to have a conscience is rather the most primordial existentiell presupposition for the possibility of factically coming to owe something. — Heidegger, *Being and Time,* 334 (288).

(4) When Dasein understandingly lets itself be called forth to this possibility, this includes its *becoming free* for the call — its readiness for the potentiality of getting appealed to. In understanding the call, Dasein is *in thrall to its ownmost possibility of existence.* It has chosen itself. — Heidegger, *Being and Time,* 334 (287).

(5) Heidegger writes that solicitude, considered positively, has two aspects. First, solicitude is able to

leap in for him. This kind of solicitude takes over for the Other that with which he is to concern himself. The Other is thus thrown out of his own position; he steps back so that afterwards, when the matter has been attended to, he can either take it over as something finished and at his disposal, or disburden himself of it completely. In such solicitude the Other can become one who is dominated and dependent, even if this domination is a tacit one and remains hidden from him.

In other words, the first kind of solicitude or concern for someone else deprives him of his freedom. It takes over from him, and he is displaced. By contrast, the second kind of solicitude is one which will

leap ahead of him in his existentiell potentiality-for-Being, not in order to take away his 'care' but rather to give it back to him authentically as such for the first time. This kind of solicitude pertains essentially to authentic care — that is, to the existence of the Other, not to a *"what"* with which he is concerned; it helps the Other to become transparent to himself *in* his care and to become *free* for it. — Heidegger, *Being and Time,* 158, 159 (122).

58

(6) The more authentically Dasein resolves — and this means that in anticipating death it understands itself unambiguously in terms of its ownmost distinctive possibility — the more unequivocally does it choose and find the possibility of its existence, and the less does it do so by accident. Only by the anticipation of death is every accidental and 'provisional' possibility driven out. . . . Dasein *hands* itself *down* to itself, free for death, in a possibility which it has inherited and yet has chosen. — Heidegger, *Being and Time,* 435 (384).

(7) Being-free *for* one's ownmost potentiality-for-Being, and therewith for the possibility of authenticity and inauthenticity, is shown, with a primordial, elemental concreteness, in anxiety. — Heidegger, *Being and Time,* 236 (191).

(8) Only if death, guilt, conscience, freedom, and finitude reside together equiprimordially in the Being of an entity as they do in care, can that entity exist in the mode of fate; that is to say, only then can it be historical in the very depths of its existence. — Heidegger, *Being and Time,* 437 (385).

6. Jean-Paul Sartre's doctrine of freedom, as has been observed is the most radical such doctrine to appear thus far in philosophical thought. Sartre wants men to accept their own absolute responsibility for their lives. Thus he opposes any reliance upon the divine. All of man's alibis are unacceptable: no gods are responsible for man's condition, no original sin, no heredity or environment, no race, no caste, no father, no mother, no wrong-headed education, no impulse or disposition, no complex, no childhood trauma. Man is free, completely free. Man is *condemned* to be free.

(1) We were never more free than during the German occupation. We had lost all our rights, beginning with the right to talk. Every day we were insulted to our faces and had to take it in silence. Under one pretext or another, as workers, Jews, or political prisoners, we were deported

en masse. Everywhere, on billboards, in the newspapers, on the screen, we encountered the revolting and insipid picture of ourselves that our oppressors wanted us to accept. And, because of all this, we were free. Because the Nazi venom seeped even into our thoughts, every accurate thought was a conquest. Because an all-powerful police tried to force us to hold our tongues, every word took on the value of a declaration of principles. . . . Exile, captivity, and especially death (which we usually shrink from facing at all in happier times) became for us the habitual objects of our concern. We learned that they were neither inevitable accidents, nor even constant and exterior dangers, but that they must be considered as our lot itself, our destiny, the profound source of our reality as men. — Jean-Paul Sartre, *The Republic of Silence.*

(2) We have shown that freedom is actually one with the being of the For-itself; human reality is free to the exact extent that it has to be its own nothingness. It has to be this nothingness, as we have seen, in multiple dimensions: first, by temporalizing itself — i.e., by being always at a distance from itself, which means that it can never let itself be determined by its past to perform this or that particular act; second, by rising up as consciousness of something and (of) itself — i.e., by being presence to itself and not simply self, which implies that nothing exists in consciousness which is not consciousness of existing and that consequently nothing external to consciousness can motivate it; and finally, by being transcendence — i.e., not something which would first be in order subsequently to put itself into relation with this or that end, but on the contrary, a being which is originally a project — i.e., which is defined by its end. — Sartre, *Being and Nothingness,* 429.

(3) It is necessary to point out to "common sense" that the formula "to be free" does not mean "to obtain what one has wished" (in the broad sense of choosing). In other words success is not important to freedom. . . . Thus we shall not say that a prisoner is always free to go out of

60

prison, which would be absurd, nor that he is always free to long for release, which would be an irrelevant truism, but that he is always free to try to escape (or get himself liberated); that is, that whatever his condition may be, he can project his escape and learn the value of his project by undertaking some action. Our description of freedom, since it does not distinguish between choosing and doing, compels us to abandon at once the distinction between the intention and the act. The intention can no more be separated from the act than thought can be separated from the language which expresses it. — Sartre, *Being and Nothingness,* 459, 460.

(4) Thus we begin to catch a glimpse of the paradox of freedom: there is freedom only in a *situation,* and there is a situation only through freedom. — Sartre, *Being and Nothingness,* 465.

(5) This is certainly one of the meanings which Kafka's *The Trial* tries to bring to light, the characteristics in human reality of being perpetually *in court.* To be free is to *have one's freedom perpetually on trial.* — Sartre, *Being and Nothingness,* 478.

(6) These external limits of freedom, precisely because they are external and are interiorized only as unrealizables, will never be either a *real* obstacle for freedom or a limit suffered. Freedom is total and infinite, which does not mean that it has no limits but that it *never encounters them.* The only limits which freedom bumps up against at each moment are those which it imposes on itself and of which we have spoken in connection with the past, with the environment, and with techniques. — Sartre, *Being and Nothingness,* 507.

7. Gabriel Marcel writes that:
Freedom has no choice but to affirm itself, by faith, a stranger to death, just as it is alien to time. — Marcel, *Philosophical Fragments,* 96.

8. Nicolas Berdyaev comments:

(1) Freedom may lead man to evil; it is tragic in character and does not come under any pedagogical or morally legalistic categories. Freedom is the essential condition of moral life — freedom in evil as well as in good. — Berdyaev, *The Destiny of Man,* 19.

(2) A true consciousness of guilt would set man free. — Berdyaev, *Slavery and Freedom,* 62.

(3) Freedom which has been established by an habitual way of living, passes over into an unnoticed enslavement of men; this is freedom which has become objectivized, whereas all the while freedom is the realm of the subject. Man is a slave because freedom is difficult, whereas slavery is easy. — Berdyaev, *Slavery and Freedom,* 66.

(4) The relation between personality and God is not a causal relation, it lies outside the realm of determination, it is within the realm of freedom, God is not an object to personality. He is a subject. — Berdyaev, *Slavery and Freedom,* 26.

(5) God does not act in the determined arrangement of things which belongs to objectivized nature. He acts only in freedom, only through the freedom of man. — Berdyaev, *Slavery and Freedom,* 263.

(6) The way of liberation lies on the other side of traditional immanence and transcendence. The process of transcension in freedom never means subjection to an alien will, which indeed is slavery, but subjection to the Truth which is at the same time also the Way and the Life. — Berdyaev, *Slavery and Freedom,* 70.

9. Viktor Frankl, the leading psychological existentialist, reflects on the meaning of freedom from a psychological point of view:

In this connection I would like to stress the difference between freedom and responsibility, for the neglect of this difference seems to me to be the main mistake of so-called existentialism. Freedom means freedom from something; whereas responsibility, in contrast, involves a twofold reference to the world, insofar as man is always responsible (1) for something and (2) to something. What he is responsible for is the specific meaning to be fulfilled by him, the specific values to be actualized by him. The question of what he is responsible to cannot be answered in a general way, at least not by a psychotherapist. This question must be answered in the most personal way, and a psychotherapist should be the last to let the patient escape his responsibility for answering such a personal question. It is up to the patient himself to decide whether he will consider himself responsible to society, or to his conscience, or to God whom he feels standing behind this conscience. At any rate, the religious man could be defined as one who actually does not feel responsible to something, but to someone. He does not interpret his life only in terms of a task but also in terms of a task master. — Frankl, *From Death Camp to Existentialism*, 108.

10.   Paul Tillich, the leading theological existentialist, provides a characteristically balanced summary of thought about freedom in its broad outline.

Man, in so far as he sets and pursues purposes, is free. He transcends the given situation, leaving the real for the sake of the possible. He is not bound to the situation in which he finds himself, and it is just this self-transcendence that is the first and basic quality of freedom. Therefore, no historical situation determines any other historical situation completely. The transition from one situation to another is in part determined by man's centered action, by his freedom. According to the polarity of freedom and destiny, such self-transcendence is not absolute; it comes out of the totality of elements of past and present, but within these limits it is able to produce something qualitatively new. — Tillich, *Systematic Theology*, III, 303.

FUTURE: (Latin *futurus,* about to be, future particle of *esse,* to be)

1. Time is the central category of finitude. Every philosopher has been fascinated and embarrassed by its mysterious character. Some philosophers emphasize the negative element; others, the positive element. The former point to the transitoriness of everything temporal and to the impossibility of fixing the present moment within a flux of time which never stands still. They point to the movement of time from a past that is no more toward a future that is not yet through a present which is nothing more than the moving boundary line between past and future. To be means to be present. But if the present is illusory, being is conquered by nonbeing. — Paul Tillich, *Systematic Theology,* I, 193.

2. It is surely naïve and undialectical to let oneself get enthusiastic at the thought of a better future, a future when one will be understood better — as though things did not always remain essentially the same, namely, bad, or if there is a change then it is for the worse.

   A better future, and better understood — that means a future in which admiring professorial rascals and priestly riffraff turn the dead man's life and work and witness into profit for themselves and their families. Is this a better future? Is this to be better understood? — Søren Kierkegaard, *The Last Years,* 197.

3. Well! The lion hath come, my children are nigh, Zarathustra hath grown ripe, mine hour hath come: —
   This is *my* morning, *my* day beginneth: *arise now, arise, thou great noontide!* — Friedrich Nietzsche, *Thus Spake Zarathustra,* 368.

4. (German *Zukunft*) This letting-itself-*come-towards*-itself in that distinctive possibility which it puts up with, is the primordial, phenomenon of the *future as coming towards.*
   . . . By the term 'futural', we do not here have in view a "now" which has *not yet* become 'actual' and which some-

64

time *will* be for the first time. We have in view the coming [*Kunft*] in which Dasein, in its ownmost potentiality-for-Being, comes towards itself. Anticipation makes Dasein *authentically* futural, and in such a way that the anticipation itself is possible only in so far as Dasein, *as being,* always coming towards itself — that is to say, in so far as it is futural in its Being in general. — Martin Heidegger, *Being and Time,* 372, 373 (325).

5. There are two sorts of Future: the one is but the temporal ground on which my present perception develops, the other is posited for itself but as that which is not yet. — Jean-Paul Sartre, *The Psychology of Imagination.*

6. The future is what the For-itself has to be. It is "The determining being which the For-itself has to be beyond being." — Sartre, *Being and Nothingness,* 550.

7. We should concern ourselves only with that part of the future on which we have a hold. But we should try our best to enlarge our hold on it as much as possible. — Simone de Beauvoir, *All Men Are Mortal.*

8. It is a peculiarity of man that he can only live by looking to the future — *sub specie aeternitatis.* And this is his salvation in the most difficult moments of his existence, although he sometimes has to force his mind to the task.

I remember a personal experience. Almost in tears from pain (I had terrible sores on my feet from wearing torn shoes), I limped a few kilometers with our long column of men from the camp to our work site. Very cold, bitter winds struck us. I kept thinking of the endless little problems of our miserable life. What would there be to eat tonight? If a piece of sausage came as extra ration, should I exchange it for a piece of bread? Should I trade my last cigarette, which was left from a bonus I received a fortnight ago, for a bowl of soup? How could I get a piece of wire to replace the fragment which served as one of my shoelaces? Would I get to our work site in time to join my usual working party or would I have to join another, which might have a brutal foreman? What could I do to get on good terms with the Capo, who could help me obtain work in camp instead of undertaking this horribly long daily march?

I became disgusted with the state of affairs which compelled me, daily and hourly, to think of only such trivial things. I forced my thoughts to turn to another subject. Suddenly I saw myself standing on the platform of a well-lit, warm and pleasant lecture room. In front of me sat an attentive audience on comfortable upholstered seats. I was giving a lecture on the psychology of the concentration camp! All that oppressed me at that moment became objective, seen and described from the remote viewpoint of science. By this method I succeeded somehow in rising above the situation, above the sufferings of the moment, and I observed them as if they were already of the past. Both I and my troubles became the object of an interesting psychoscientific study undertaken by myself. What does Spinoza say in his *Ethics?* — *"Affectus, qui passio est, desinit esse passio simlatque eius claram et distinctam formamus ideam."* Emotion, which is suffering, ceases to be suffering as soon as we form a clear and precise picture of it. — Viktor Frankl, *From Death Camp to Existentialism,* 74.

9. "What is the relation of eternity to the modes of time?" An answer demands use of the only analogy to eternity found in human experience, that is, the unity of remembered past and anticipated future in an experienced present. Such an analogy implies a symbolic approach to the meaning of eternity. In accord with the predominance of the present in temporal experience, eternity must first be symbolized as an eternal present *(nunc eternum).* But this *nunc eternum* is not simultaneity or the negation of an independent meaning of past and future. The eternal present is moving from past to future but without ceasing to be present. The future is genuine only if it is open, if the new can happen and if it can be anticipated. — Tillich, *Systematic Theology,* I, 175.

G

GOD: (etymology uncertain: Gothic *guth,* god, probably akin to Old Irish *guth,* voice, and to Greek *kauchasthai,* to boast; probably from the Indo-European base *ghawa-, to call out, to invoke)

Existential philosophers are divided into atheistic and theistic schools of thought, according to Sartre. The atheistic existentialists are Nietzsche, Sartre and the French school of existentiallism, and Heidegger. The theistic existentialists are Kierkegaard, Jaspers, and Tillich. More important than this formal division is each thinker's conception of God and the place assigned to God within his thought. For example, Kierkegaard assigns a central role to God throughout his works, including his epistemology. Sartre, on the other hand, consciously excludes God from his philosophy, although his definition of God is one which would be as unsatisfactory for Tillich as it is for Sartre.

1. Friedrich Nietzsche wrote of "the death of God," by which he meant the loss of the culture's base of values. This loss was fundamentally good, in Nietzsche's view, because it makes way for the will to power which in turn leads to the creation of new values. Culminating these new values will be the superman or over-man *(übermensch).*

Have you not heard of that madman who lit a lantern in the bright morning hours, ran to the market place, and cried incessantly, "I seek God! I seek God!" As many of those who do not believe in God were standing around just then, he provoked much laughter. Why, did he get lost? said one. Did he lose his way like a child? said another.

Or is he hiding? Is he afraid of us? Has he gone on a voyage? or emigrated? Thus they yelled and laughed. The madman jumped into their midst and pierced them with his glances.

"Whither is God" he cried. "I shall tell you. *We have killed him* — you and I. All of us are his murderers. But how have we done this? How were we able to drink up the sea? Who gave us the sponge to wipe away the entire horizon? What did we do when we unchained this earth from its sun? Whither is it moving now? Whither are we moving now? Away from all suns? Are we not plunging continually? Backward, sideward, forward, in all directions? Is there any up or down left? Are we not straying as through an infinite nothing? Do we not feel the breath of empty space? Has it not become colder? Is not night and more night coming on all the while? Must not lanterns be lit in the morning? Do we not hear anything yet of the noise of the grave-diggers who are burying God? Do we not smell anything yet of God's decomposition? Gods too decompose.

God is dead. God remains dead. And we have killed him. How shall we, the murderers of all murderers, comfort ourselves? What was holiest and most powerful of all that the world has yet owned has bled to death under our knives. Who will wipe this blood off us? What water is there for us to clean ourselves? What festivals of atonement, what sacred games shall we have to invent? Is not the greatness of this deed too great for us? Must not we ourselves become gods simply to seem worthy of it? There has never been a greater deed; and whoever will be born after us — for the sake of this deed he will be part of a higher history than all history hitherto."

Here the madman fell silent and looked again at his listeners; and they too were silent and stared at him in astonishment. At last he threw his lantern on the ground, and it broke and went out. "I come too early," he said then; "my time has not come yet. This tremendous event is still on its way, still wandering — it has not yet reached the ears of man. Lightning and thunder require time, the light of the stars requires time, deeds require time even after they are done, before they can be seen and heard. This deed is still more distant from them than the most distant stars —*and yet they have done it themselves.*"

It has been related further that on that same day the madman entered divers churches and there sang his *requiem aeternam deo.* Led out and called to account, he is said to have replied each time, "What are these churches now if they are not the tombs and sepulchers of God?"—Nietzsche, in Kaufmann, *Existentialism from Dostoevsky to Sartre,* 105, 106.

2. Jean-Paul Sartre, who also speaks of the death of God, means that it is necessary for man to invent his own values, to freely choose oneself as an image of man for all men.

(1)   The existentialist, on the contrary, finds it extremely embarrassing that God does not exist, for there disappears with Him all possibility of finding values in an intelligible heaven. There can no longer be any good *a priori,* since there is no infinite and perfect consciousness to think it. It is nowhere written that "the good" exists, that one must be honest or must not lie, since we are now upon the plane where there are only men. Dostoevsky once wrote "If God did not exist, everything would be permitted"; and that, for existentialism, is the starting point. Everything is indeed permitted if God does not exist, and man is in consequence forlorn, for he cannot find anything to depend upon either within or outside himself. He discovers forthwith, that he is without excuse.—Jean-Paul Sartre, "Existentialism", in *Existentialism from Dostoevsky to Sartre,* 294, 295.

(2)   Existentialism is not atheistic in the sense that it would exhaust itself in demonstrations of the non-existence of God. It declares, rather, that even if God existed that it would make no difference from its point of view. Not that we believe God does exist, but we think that the real problem is not that of His existence; what man needs is to find him-

self again and to understand that nothing can save him from himself, not even a valid proof of the existence of God. — Sartre, *ibid.*, 311.

(3) Hilda: Did you win your case?

Goetz: There was no trial: I tell you, God is dead. [He takes her in his arms.]
We have no witness now, I alone can see your hair and your brow. How REAL you have become since He no longer exists. Look at me, don't stop looking at me for one moment: the world has been struck blind; if you turned away your head, I should be afraid of annihilation. [He laughs.] . . . .

Goetz: Heinrich, I am going to tell you a colossal joke: God doesn't exist. . . .

Goetz: I alone. I supplicated, I demanded a sign. I sent messages to Heaven, no reply. Heaven ignored my very name. Each minute I wondered what I could BE in the eyes of God. Now I know the answer: nothing. God does not see me, God does not hear me, God does not know me. You see this gap in the door? It is God. You see that hole in the ground? That is God again. Silence is God. Absence is God. God is the loneliness of man. . . .

Goetz: There was no one but myself; I alone decided on Evil; and I alone invented Good. It was I who cheated, I who worked miracles, I who accused myself today, I alone who can absolve myself; I, man. If God exists, man is nothing; if man exists. . . .

—Sartre, *The Devil and the Good Lord.*

(4) Orestes: What do I care for Zeus? Justice is a matter between men, and I need no god to teach it to me.

Zeus: Orestes, I created you, and I created all things. Now see!

[The walls of the temple draw apart, revealing the firmament, spangled with wheeling stars. ZEUS is standing in the background. His voice becomes huge — amplified by loud-speakers — but his form is shadowy.]

See those planets wheeling on their appointed ways, never swerving, never clashing. It was I who ordained their courses, according to the law of justice. Hear the music of the spheres, that vast, mineral hymn of praise, sounding and resounding to the limits of the firmament. [Sounds of music]. It is my work that living things increase and multiply, each according to his kind. . . .

Impudent spawn! So I am not your king? Who, then, made you?

Orestes: You. But you blundered; you should not have made me free. . . . I *am* my freedom. No sooner had you created me than I ceased to be yours . . . .

You are God and I am free; each of us is alone, and our anguish is akin. . . . Human life begins on the far side of despair. [A short silence]

Zeus: Well, Orestes, all this was foreknown. In the fullness of time a man was to come, to announce my decline. And you're that man, it seems.

— Sartre, *The Flies.*

3. Martin Heidegger, when he writes about the death of God, does not mean Nietzsche's void which can be filled by a "superman", but rather the occasion for a new succession of divine images arising from man's clarifying thoughts about being.

It is the time of the gods that have fled *and* of the god that is coming. It is the time of *need,* because it lies under a double lack and a double Not: the No-more of the gods that have fled and the Not-yet of the god that is coming. — Heidegger, in Michalson, *Christianity and the Existentialists,* 169.

4. Martin Buber, another of the existentialists who writes of the death of God, means the *eclipse* of God. This eclipse occurs when man turns away from God by allowing the "I-It" relationship to predominate. The cause of the eclipse is that God answers this situation by seeming to be absent himself.

5. Sǿren Kierkegaard, the first of the theistic existentialists (chronologically), also rejects the validity of formal proofs of God. He argues that one should reason *from* existence rather than *toward* it. Existence is never subject to demonstration.

(1) I always reason from existence, not toward existence, whether I move in the sphere of palpable sensible fact or in the realm of thought. I do not for example prove that a stone exists, but that some existing thing is a stone. The procedure in a court of justice does not prove that a criminal exists, but that the accused, whose existence is given, is a criminal. Whether we call existence an *accessorium* or the eternal *prius,* it is never subject to demonstration. — Kierkegaard (Johannes Climacus), *Philosophical Framents,* 50.

(2) My development, or any man's, proceeds like this: Maybe he too starts out with some reasons, but they represent the lower plane. Then he makes a choice; under the weight of responsibility before God a conviction will be born in him by God's help. Now he has attained the positive. Henceforth he cannot defend his conviction or prove it by reasons; that would be a contradiction in terms, since reasons belong to the lower plane. No, the matter becomes further personal, or it becomes a question of personality, i.e. one can only defend one's conviction ethically, personally, that is through the sacrifices one is willing to make for it and by the dauntlessness with which one maintains it.

There is only one proof of the truth of Christianity: the

inner proof, *argumentum spiritus sancti.* — Kierkegaard, *The Diary,* 164.

(3)   The best proof of the soul's immortality, that God exists, etc., actually is the impression one received thereof in childhood, namely the proof which, differing from the many learned and grandiloquent proofs, could be summarized thus: It is absolutely true, because my father told me so. — Kierkegaard, *The Diary,* 34.

6.   Karl Jaspers writes:

But when for lack of firm ground we become dizzy — and the extreme seems still to lie ahead of us — then it is true that when everything goes under, God remains. It is true that there is transcendence.
Not even Europe is the last thing for us. We become Europeans on condition that we really become men — that is, men from the depths of the origin and the goal, both of which lie in God. — Jaspers, *The European Spirit,* 64.

7.   Nicolas Berdyaev also grants an important place to the doctrine of God in his writings:

It is impossible to pass judgment on God, for He is the source of all the values by reference to which we judge. — Berdyaev, *The Destiny of Man,* 43.

It is obvious that God is "beyond good and evil", for on "this side" of it is our fallen world and certainly not God. God is above good. — Berdyaev, *ibid.*

8.   Paul Tillich writes of the necessity of going to the "God beyond God," to the "ground of Being," which is superior to both mysticism and theism.

(1)   God does not exist. He is being-itself beyond essence and existence. Therefore, to argue that God exists is to deny him. — Tillich, *Systematic Theology,* I, 205.

(2)   "God" is the answer to the question implied in man's finitude; he is the name for that which concerns man ultimately. This does not mean that first there is a being

called God and then the demand that man should be ultimately becomes god for him, and, conversely, it means that a man can be concerned ultimately only about that which is god for him.— Tillich, *ibid.*, 211.

(3) God is the answer to the question implied in human finitude. This answer cannot be derived from the analysis of existence. However, if the notion of God appears in systematic theology in correlation with the threat of nonbeing which is implied in existence, God must be called the infinite power of being which resists the threat of nonbeing. In classical theology this is being-itself. If anxiety is defined as the awareness of being finite, God must be called the infinite ground of courage. In classical theology this is universal providence. If the notion of the Kingdom of God appears in correlation with the riddle of our historical existence, it must be called the meaning, fulfilment, and unity of history. In this way an interpretation of the traditional symbols of Christianity is achieved which preserves the power of these symbols and which opens them to the questions elaborated by our present analysis of human existence. — Tillich, *ibid.*, 64.

(4) The religious word for what is called the ground of being is God. — Tillich, *ibid.*, 156.

(5) The divine life is the dynamic unity of depth and form. In mystical language the depth of the divine life, its inexhaustible and ineffable character, is called "Abyss." In philosophical language the form, the meaning and structure element of the divine life, is called "Logos." In religious language the dynamic unity of both elements is called "Spirit." Tillich, *ibid.*, 156.

(6) If God is brought into the subject-object structure of being, he ceases to be the ground of being and becomes one being among others (first of all, a being beside the subject who looks at him as an object). He ceases to be the God who is really God. — Tillich, *ibid.*, 172.

(7) Spirit is the unity of the ontological elements and the *telos* of life. Actualized as life, being-itself is fulfilled as

74

spirit. The word *telos* expresses the relation of life and spirit more precisely than the words "aim" or "goal." It expresses the inner directedness of life toward spirit, the urge of life to become spirit, to fulfil itself as spirit. *Telos* stands for an inner, essential, necessary aim, for that in which a being fulfils its own nature. God as living is God fulfilled in himself and therefore spirit. God *is* spirit. This is the most embracing, direct, and unrestricted symbol for the divine life. It does not need to be balanced with another symbol, because it includes all the ontological elements. — Tillich, *ibid.,* 249.

(8) The ultimate source of the courage to be is the "God above God"; this is the result of our demand to transcend theism. Only if the God of theism is transcended can the anxiety of doubt and meaninglessness be taken into the courage to be. . . . *The courage to be is rooted in the God who appears when God has disappeared in the anxiety of doubt.* — Tillich, *The Courage to Be,* 186, 190.

GOOD: (from the Sanskrit *gadh,* to hold fast, uniting or fitting together)

The individual is the only center for the choice of the good. No rules or commandments or laws have any ethical significance unless they are chosen by the individual. This choice is completely free. Man is free to choose his own nature. Man alone is responsible to choose what he is to become, and this is his choice alone. Objective advice on moral matters cannot be given, as choice and value are subjective.

1. Kierkegaard defines ethics almost in a Kantian manner. Then he states that the ethical is merely the second of three spheres of existence, or stages on life's way.

It is no use arguing with ethics, for ethics has pure categories. It does not appeal to experience, which of all ludicrous things is the most ludicrous, and which so far from making a man wise rather makes him mad if he knows nothing higher than this. — Johannes de silentio (Søren Kierkegaard), *Fear and Trembling*, 95.

This formal definition of the good is a priori, universal and necessary, and before experience of any sort. However, Kierkegaard immediately adds to this idealistic definition a qualification which indicates that the decisive thing is the individual's relation to the good. We might say that the ethical problem is not to understand the good, but to do it.

Ethics has in its possession no chance, and so matters do not come to an explanation, it does not joke about serious matters, it lays a heavy responsibility on the shoulders of the tiny hero. It denounces as pride his wish to play providence by his actions. It also denounces him for wishing to do it by his own suffering. It commands a man to believe in reality and to have the courage to fight against all the troubles of reality. — *Ibid.*

After defining the ethical as the science of the ideal, with pure categories which are prior to experience, and after adding that the problem in ethics is not so much to understand the good as to do it, Kierkegaard states that the ethical is merely the second of the three spheres of existence, the three stages on life's way.

The first stage is the "esthetic". This is the choice of pleasure, the enjoyment of life, the seduction of women, whether as Don Juan, who sees women as nothing more than a succession of vaginas, or as Casanova, who sees women as unique and fascinating personalities. The inescapable problem which arises from the pursuit of pleasure is boredom. In the attempt to escape this boredom one will seek to refine his pleasures or to alternate them, as in "the rotation method." The pleasure-seeker attempts to prolong the process of acquiring the pleasure for as long as possible. Thus the pleasure is more in the pursuit than in the actual conquest.

By the aid of his intellectual endowments he had known how to tempt a young girl and attract her to himself, without really caring to possess her. I can imagine that he knew how to excite a girl to the highest pitch, so that he was

76

certain that she was ready to sacrifice everything. When the affair reached this point, he broke it off without himself having let fall a single word of love, let alone a declaration, a promise. — Victor Eremita (Søren Kierkegaard), *Either/ Or,* 302, 303.

The intermediary rung between the esthetic and the ethical stages is irony, the sign of a greatly widened awareness of the character of existence.

The second stage on life's way is the ethical. This stage is best represented by Judge William's essay on marriage. A woman, he says, does not live for a single climactic moment. Rather, her beauty increases with the passing years. The steady responsibilities of the marital state provide the best example of the union of personal inclination and social duty. One accepts his own personal duty, eliminates all wishful thinking and becomes the true medium of the universal. This is the choice of oneself. This, incidentally, provides a correction of the Kantian separation of duty from inclination. Duty, in this view, is not moral law, as it was for Kant. Rather, duty is an inward summons. It is always *my* duty.

The problem which arises in the ethical sphere is guilt. One recognizes the gap between duty and performance. This gap cannot be bridged, and the ethical stage remains incomplete. One way of stating this is: "Against God we are always in the wrong." — *Ibid.,* 355.

The transition rung between the ethical and the religious stages is humor. Humor is the sign of the self-assured individual who is able to accept life's situations.

The third stage, then, is the religious. The ethical is suspended — the "teleological suspension of the ethical" — in view of the individual's higher relation to God. The idea is that "the particular stands in an absolute relation to the absolute, "and as such is "superior to the universal." — Johannes de silentio (Søren Kierkegaard), *Fear and Trembling,* 66.

The illustration of this is the case of Abraham, when he was required to sacrifice his son Isaac. This requirement was to break the moral code forbidding murder. This higher religious demand was not "universal" in the sense in which the ethical code is universal, because Abraham's relation to God is a private relation. Abraham's suspension of the ethical consciousness is the result of his private and individual relationship with God. Abraham speaks cryptically because he has put himself beyond the universal sphere of reference. His actions are justified only because they are acts of faith.

The religious stage is divided into two parts: "Religiousness A" and "Religiousness B." They are not two separate stages because you can never have one without the other. "Religiousness A" is general religiousness. It is romantic and immanent. God is everywhere, and, therefore, God is nowhere in a concrete or specific sense. It is paganism but without the saving simplicity of true paganism. It is also philosophical, European since Descartes. The mob tends to be canonized. It is Christian in the vague sense of "Christendom." Religiousness A has never brought a true man into being, and has never given man a true self by itself. — Johannes Climacus, *Concluding Unscientific Postscript,* 507.

"Religiousness B" is the Christian revelation characterized by the God-Man paradox. This paradox, that one individual was both fully human and fully divine, is an offence to the reason. However, the paradox is also an atonement, through which God brings "repetition" to man, restoring man to equilibrium and to himself.

2. Nietzsche writes with contempt for the "good" as conceived by Christian civilization. Such values as pity and compassion must be overthrown and "trans-valued" into the higher virtues of the super-man.

Nobody, up to now, has doubted that the "good" man represents a higher value than the "evil," in terms of promoting and benefiting mankind generally, even taking the long view. But suppose the exact opposite were true. What if the "good" man represents not merely a retrogression but even a danger, a temptation, a narcotic drug enabling the present to live at the expense of the future? More comfortable, less hazardous, perhaps, but also baser, more petty —

so that morality itself would be responsible for man, as a species, failing to reach the peak of magnificence of which he is capable? What if morality should turn out to be the danger of dangers? — Friedrich Nietzsche, *The Genealogy of Morals,* 155.

To answer the question he raises about the validity of moral systems, Nietzsche proposes an investigation into the history of the formation of such notions of good.

"Under what conditions did man construct the value judgments *good* and *evil?"* And what is their intrinsic worth? Have they thus far benefited or retarded mankind? Do they betoken misery, curtailment, degeneracy or, on the contrary, power, fullness of being, energy, courage in the face of life, and confidence in the future? A great variety of answers suggested themselves. I began to distinguish among periods, nations, individuals; I narrowed the problem down; the answers grew into new questions, investigations, suppositions, probabilities, until I had staked off at last my own domain, a whole hidden, growing and blooming world, secret gardens as it were, of whose existence no one must have an inkling. . . . How blessed are we knowers, provided we know to keep silent long enough! — *Ibid.,* 152.

The answer which develops, according to Nietzsche, is that "good" and "evil" had a double evolution, in the ruling class and in the slave class respectively.

The conception of good and evil has a twofold early history, namely, *once* in the soul of the ruling tribes and castes. Whoever has the power of returning good for good, evil for evil, and really practises requital, and who is, therefore, grateful and revengeful, is called good; whoever is powerless, and unable to requite, is reckoned as bad. As a good man is reckoned among the "good," a community which has common feelings because the single individuals are bound to one another by the sense of requital. As a bad man one belongs to the "bad," to a party of subordinate, powerless people who have no common feeling. The good are a caste, the bad are a mass like dust. Good and bad have for a long time meant the same thing as noble and base, master and slave. On the other hand, the enemy is not looked upon as evil, he can requite. In Homer the Trojan and the Greek are both good. It is not the one who injures us, but the one who is despicable, who is called bad. Good is inherited in the community of the good; it is impossible that a bad man could spring from such good soil. If, nevertheless, one of the good ones does something which is unworthy of the good, refuge is sought in excuses; the guilt is thrown upon a god, for instance; it is said that he has struck the good man with blindness and madness.

Then in the soul of the oppressed and powerless. Here every *other* man is looked upon as hostile, inconsiderate, rapacious, cruel, cunning, be he noble or base; evil is the distinguishing word for man, even for every conceivable living creature, *e.g.* for a god; human, divine, is the same thing as devilish, evil. The signs of goodness, helpfulness, pity, are looked upon with fear as spite, the prelude to a terrible result, stupefaction and outwitting, — in short, as refined malice. With such a disposition in the individual a community could hardly exist, or at most it could exist only in its crudest form, so that in all places where this conception of good and evil obtains, the downfall of the single individuals, of their tribes and races, is at hand. Our present civilization has grown up on the soil of the *ruling* tribes and castes. — Friedrich Nietzsche, *Human, All-too-Human,* 65, 66.

In a similar way, Nietzsche considers the origin of Justice to be a mutual adjustment between roughly equal powers. Balance is the precondition of all contracts and covenants, and hence of all law. On the basis of this analysis, with current moral codes the results of previous social conditions, Nietzsche calls for a reformulation of values:

But today — shouldn't we have reached the necessity of once more resolving on a reversal and fundamental shift in values, owing to another self-examination of man, another growth in profundity? Don't we stand at the threshold of a period which should be designated negatively, to begin with, as *extra-moral?* After all, today at least we immoralists have the suspicion that the decisive value of an action lies precisely in what is *unintentional* in it. . . . The overcoming of morality, in a certain sense even the self-overcoming of morality — let this be the name for that long secret work which has been saved up for the finest and most honest, also the most malicious, consciences of today, as living touchstones of the soul. — Friedrich Nietzsche, *Beyond Good and Evil,* 44, 45.

Specifically, the values of Christian civilization, values such as purity, humility, and unselfishness must be overthrown and replaced by a new order of virtues:

The great epochs of our life come when we gain the courage to rechristen our evil as what is best in us. — Nietzsche, *Beyond Good and Evil,* 86.

Do I advise you to love your neighbor? Rather do I advise you to flee from your neighbor and love what is farthest!

Higher than love of your neighbor is love of the farthest and future ones; higher still than love of men is love of things and phantoms. — Nietzsche, *Thus Spake Zarathustra,* 63.

Voluptuousness, passion for power, and *selfishness:* these three things have hitherto been best cursed, and have been in worst and falsest repute — these three things will I weigh humanly well. — *Ibid.,* 208.

And then it happened also, — and verily, it happened for the first time! — that his word blessed *selfishness,* the wholesome, healthy selfishness, that springeth from the powerful soul:

. . . From the powerful soul, to which the high body appertaineth, the handsome, triumphing, refreshing body, around which everything becometh a mirror:

. . . The pliant, persuasive body, the dancer, whose symbol and epitome is the self-enjoying soul. Of such bodies and souls the self-enjoyment calleth itself "virtue." — *Ibid.,* 211.

Christianity gave Eros poison to drink: he did not die of

it but degenerated — into a vice. — Nietzsche, *Beyond Good and Evil*, 92.

When the old virtues of Christianity have been replaced by the new virtues of the super-man, then a courageous new type of life will be ready to begin, for "Whatever is done from love always occurs beyond good and evil." — *Ibid.*, 90.

3. Berdyaev rejects the various attempts to subject the individual to some external authority, whether of the old morality or of the new immorality:

The ethics of law is the expression of herd morality. It organizes the life of the average man, of the human herd, and leaves altogether out of account the creative human personality which rises above the common level. It deals with personality in the abstract; the concrete person does not exist for it. — Nicolas Berdyaev, *The Destiny of Man*, 91.

Berdyaev does not share Nietzsche's optimism that once the old values are gone they will be replaced by better values. From the perspective of the social disasters of the first half of the twentieth century, Berdyaev writes:

We live in a time when men neither love nor seek the truth. In ever greater measure, truth is being replaced by the will to power, by what is useful or valuable to special interests. This lack of love for the truth appears not only in nihilistic or sceptic attitudes toward it, but in substituting for it some sort of falsehood which is considered not evil, but good. . . . And if our times are distinguished by an exceptional tendency to lying, it is a special sort of untruth. Falsehood is affirmed as some holy duty for the sake of higher purposes. Evil is justified in the name of good. — Berdyaev, *The Realm of Spirit and the Realm of Caesar*, 13.

4. Jaspers, in his explanation of what he calls "philosophical faith", states the importance of

the realization of the absolute nature of the decision between good and evil in finite man . . . (and) types of moral world order which are always historically absolute, although none of their manifestations is absolute or exclusive. — Karl Jaspers, *The Perennial Scope of Philosophy*, 107, 108.

Jaspers is critical of the straight interpretation of Nietzsche, preferring instead his own more sophisticated interpretation, by which he concludes that Nietzsche was dialectical in his intention. Thus Nietzsche is not the nihilist, but the prophet attempting to purify Christian values.

When there seems to be nothing left, then, and we ask where Nietzsche is bound, we hear from the depths of his thought two answers. The two go together:

The *first answer* completes the most monstrous negation as such: the denial of all morality and all truth comprehended as consequences of Christian morality and truthfulness, but now exposed as groundless. Over and over Nietzsche states this in the most brutal terms. . . .

Nietzsche's second answer to our question as to the ultimate destination of his thinking — (is) the answers following the radical negation. Even if his thinking appears as a self-destructive process in which no truth can last, even if the end is always nothingness, Nietzsche's own will is diametrically opposed to this nihilism. In empty space he wants to grasp the positive. His second answer is the design of the new world-view, the *Weltanschauung* which will be Christianity's heir — not in order to leave Christianity behind and forgotten, but to surpass it as man rises toward higher levels. This is a world-view in which the words, "Nothing is true, all is permitted," shall bring forth a deeper truth than any which has ever been known.

Yet the concrete realization of this answer raises some further questions. Does not Nietzsche, faltering before his own idea, always relapse into the way of his first answer — into boundless denial, into desperate assertion, into the fanaticism of pronunciamento, into the release of arbitrary license, dark urges, brute violence? Has he, who aimed at the stars and sought the impossible, become against his will a force which would unleash all devils within us? Or is all this merely the seductive surface? — Karl Jaspers, *Nietzsche and Christianity,* 82-85.

Jaspers writes that philosophical faith can be reached by keeping "constantly alert" while seeking peace of mind, by passing through nihilism to the assimilation of our tradition, seeking the purity of the sciences as a premise for the truth of our philosophy, and by seeing that reason becomes the boundless desire for communication.

Most of the refutations of Kierkegaard and Nietzsche that have been written up to now, are based on misunderstanding and constitute a kind of invitation to continue sleeping. They contribute trivial commonplaces calculated to remove the thorn that was stuck in our conscience by Kierkegaard and Nietzsche. But there can be no authentic development of philosophy in the future, that does not effect a fundamental evaluation of these two great thinkers. For in the decay of their own work and the sacrifice of their own life, they have revealed to us the irreplaceable truths. So long as we continue to indulge in a false peace of mind, they remain an indispensable summons to be alert. — Jaspers, *The Perennial Scope of Philosophy,* 172.

5. Tillich writes that ethics, which he defines as "the science of morals," has difficulty preserving its status. On the one hand the tendency is to degrade morals into a purely legal code, into "grace-less moralism," in which the transgressor of the law is guilty without hope of restoration. On the other hand the tendency in America is to consider morals nothing more than correct sexual behavior. Both of these tendencies are caricatures of ethics, says Tillich.

The good can be realized by means of two principles. The first is *agape,* love in the outgoing, charitable, Christian sense. The second is the *kairos,* or the Greek idea of "the right time," the proper time to act, or to refrain from acting.

Love is the answer to the problem of moralisms and morality. It answers the questions implied in all four confrontations of moralism and morality. Love is unconditional. There is nothing which could condition it by a higher principle. There is nothing above love. And love conditions itself. It enters every concrete situation and works for the reunion of the separated in a unique way.

Love transforms the moralisms of authority into a morality of risk. Love is creative and creativity includes risk. Love does not destroy factual authority but it liberates from the authority of a special place, from a irrational hypostatized authority. Love participates, and participation overcomes authority.

Love is the source of grace. Love accepts that which is unacceptable and love renews the old being so that it becomes a new being. Medieval theology almost identified love and grace, and rightly so, for that which makes one graceful is love. But grace is, at the same time, the love which forgives and accepts.

Nevertheless, love includes justice. Love without justice is a body without a backbone. The justice of love includes that no partner in this relation is asked to annihilate himself. The self which enters a love relation is preserved in its independence. Love includes justice to others and to oneself. Love is the solution of the problem: moralisms and morality.
— Paul Tillich, *Theology of Culture*, 145.

6. Sartre's definitions of the good vary with his three major works. In the first, *Being and Nothingness* (1943), he argues that one man's freedom represents a hopeless obstacle to another's. In the second, *Existentialism is a Humanism* (1946), he argues that it is impossible for one to choose one's own freedom without thereby choosing freedom for others as well. In the third, *Critique of Dialectical Reason* (1960), the viewpoint is that experience shows each individual that he is capable of freely intervening in the world in "praxis" (*q.v.*), which proceeds by means of the dialectical struggle to replace the present by a future which is forseen.

Being and Nothingness has been characterized as written in a mood of negative resistance. One instance of this is his rejection

85

of the objectively-minded man who still shares the "spirit of seriousness:"

> they are condemned to despair; for they discover at the same time that all human activities are equivalent (for they all tend to sacrifice man in order that the self-cause may arise) and that all are on principle doomed to failure. Thus it amounts to the same thing whether one gets drunk alone or is a leader of nations. If one of these activities takes precedence over the other, this will not be because of its real goal but because of the degree of consciousness which it possesses of its ideal goal; and in this case it will be the quietism of the solitary drunkard which will take precedence over the vain agitation of the leader of nations. — Jean-Paul Sartre, *Being and Nothingness, 545.*

Existentialism is a Humanism, written in the spirit of optimistic humanism, contains the example of a student who faced a dilemma. He had to choose between going to England to join the Free French Forces or staying near his mother to help her. His father, who was inclined to be a collaborator, was quarrelling with her. The young man's older brother had been killed in the German offensive of 1940. He was aware that his own disappearance — which might mean his death — would plunge his mother into despair. On the other hand, if he remained, every action he performed on her behalf would be certain to help her to live. If he left to fight, his every action might be totally ambiguous, might vanish like water into sand, might serve no useful purpose. He might be detained in Spain, never to reach England. He might be put doing office work in England or Algiers.

This case is taken by Sartre to illustrate a choice between two kinds of morality. On the one hand was the morality of sympathy and personal devotion. On the other hand was the morality of wider scope — national and international issues — but of more debatable validity. What are the principles which would help him make the choice?

The principles of Christian doctrine are of no help, because they advise the young man to act with charity, to love his neighbor, to deny himself for the sake of others, and to choose the harder road. The question arises, which is the harder road? To whom does one owe brotherly love, to the patriot or to the mother?

The principles of utilitarian ethics are of no help either. Which is the more useful aim, the general aim of fighting in and for the whole community, or the precise aim of helping one particular person to live?

The principles of Kantian ethics are also rejected by Sartre as an inadequate guide for concrete choice. The Kantian ethic commands us to never regard another as a means only, but only as an end. Now, if the young man remains with his mother, he will be fulfilling the moral requirement, but at the expense of using those fighting on his behalf as a means. Conversely, if he aids the combatants, he will be treating them as the end at the risk of treating his mother as a means.

Sartre concludes that the only valid ethical advice is: "You are free, therefore choose!" That is to say, one should "invent." No rule of general morality can show one what he ought to do. Man himself must bear the entire responsibility. We ourselves decide our being. This is what "abandonment" implies, and with abandonment goes anguish.

In the *Critique of Dialectical Reason* Sartre turns from the individualistic viewpoint of his preceding works to a consideration of the significance of man in society. Man's action in the world, his work, his rational intention in the material universe, is called "praxis." This Marxist term is necessarily dialectical in form. It proceeds to develop only by the clash and the resolution of contradictions. Existentialism will provide the humanizing influence in the new order, while Marxism will provide the cure for various economic ills that are the source of much human strife, Sartre concludes.

GOVERNANCE: In Kierkegaard, the term preferred by Walter Lowrie to translate the Danish *Styrelsen.* The Danish *Forsyn* is the usual term for the providence of God. *Styrelsen* means "rule" or "management," and in a religious sense means guidance from within. Thus *Forsyn* means the providence which provides, whereas *Styrelsen* means the providence which guides. This guidance, or govern-ance, is a transcendence, ruling an individual's outward circumstances and inward disposition, ruling from with-out, rather than from within, according to Kierkegaard. Kierkegaard discusses his view of providence in *Either/Or, Stages on Life's Way,* and *Edifying Discourses in Various Spirits.* Jens Himmelstrup discusses this doctrine in the thought of Kierkegaard in the *Terminologisk Ordbog,* volume 20 of Gyldendal's edition of Kierkegaard's *Sam-lede Vaerker.*

See also: Kierkegaard.

H

HEIDEGGER, MARTIN (1889-   ). One of the major philosophical existentialists, his major work is *Sein und Zeit* *(Being and Time)*, Part I, published in 1927.

Born in the Black Forest at Messkirch on the 26th of September, he was educated at Freiburg, where he was greatly influenced by Edmund Husserl, the founder of phenomenology.

In 1923 he was appointed professor of philosophy at Marburg. In 1928 he succeeded Husserl at Freiburg. During the efforts of the Nazi government to control the universities, Heidegger was named rector at Freiburg in 1933. In that capacity he made various speeches supporting National Socialism and exhorting the students to give their wholehearted allegience to the government. In 1934 he resigned and continued teaching.

In his major book, *Sein und Zeit,* Part I, he investigates the nature of being. To understand the nature of being, it is first necessary to understand the nature of human being *(Dasein)*. Human being can be properly understood only in terms of practical human concerns, man's basic situation, aims and moods. The more traditional methods of analysis in terms of substance and cause are not fruitful. Heidegger's procedure concludes that human existence is grounded in care and dread. Human efforts are brought to nothingness in death.

Although Heidegger denies that he is an existentialist, he does acknowledge the influence of Søren Kierkegaard on his thought. Heidegger's analysis is substantially identical with Kierkegaard's in stating that the existence of the thinker in becoming, in process, is decisive for a logical analysis of being.

The second part of *Sein und Zeit* was never published. Instead, a series of essays and lectures were produced, including *Was ist Metaphysic?* and *Vom Wesen des Grundes* in 1929, *Hölderlin und das Wesen der Dichtung* in 1936, *Vom Wesen der Wahrheit* in 1943, *Brief über den Humanismus* in 1947, *Holzwege* in 1949, *Einführung in die Metaphysik* in 1953, and *Vorträge und Aufsätze* in 1954.

Heidegger's method is philological in the sense that he bases metaphysical assertions on the root meanings of German and Greek words. It is important, he holds, to study the pre-socratic Greek philosophers in order to get behind the obscurities caused by the Latin terms employed by medieval thinkers.

The fundamental metaphysical question, he holds, is "Why is there something rather than nothing at all?" This question was often quoted by Paul Tillich, who was influenced by Heidegger. Fate and destiny are emphasized, especially since God is no longer a living God in the twentieth century ("Nietzsche's Wort 'Gott ist tot' ", God is dead — *Holzwege*).

Since retirement, Heidegger has lived in seclusion in a cabin in the Black Forest.

HISTORICAL MATERIALISM: Jean-Paul Sartre's term explaining part of his attitude toward Marxism. The only view of dialectical materialism which makes sense is historical materialism, that is, materialism viewed from inside the history of man's relation with matter. *Critique de la raison dialectique,* 1960; *Question de Méthode,* 1960 (*The Problem of Method,* 1964).

In his later thought, Sartre tends to see the ethical and political completion of existentialism in Marxism. This Marxism is a Marxism of a special kind, namely one which is purged of such "nineteenth-century anachronisms" as determinism, and one which incorporates the humanizing influences of existentialism with its regard for the existing individual. The conflict between individuals, rather than being due to the nature of the universe, is instead due to economic scarcity. When scarcity is overcome, conflict will also, in principle, be cured.

See also: Praxis, Sartre.

HISTORICIZE: To have a history, in the sense of becoming involved as a person in the actual world. This term is characteristic of Sartre, but the concept is central to all existential thinking. In the contrast between being and becoming, between substance and change, the key phenomenon is history. History is what presents itself to the viewer. Any attempt to ignore the element played by time in favor of a timeless essence is a distortion. Nothing can be understood that is not first approached through process. The observer, whose roots are in history, cannot ignore or overlook the conditions of his own being, which is that he is grounded in becoming.

Sartre seems to say that the individual can choose to have a history. Such other existential thinkers as Heidegger would say that the individual has a history whether he chooses to or not.

HISTORY: Becoming, or change, as opposed to being, or substance. History, according to existential thinking, is the precondition of human knowledge.

1. According to Kierkegaard, from history we learn nothing. History can give only probability, never certainty.

2. Nietzsche praises the "historical sense" which, he writes, is the only quality which will lead to effective and dominating philosophy:

The *historical sense* (or the capacity for quickly guessing the order of rank of the valuations according to which a people, a society, a human being has lived; the "divinatory instinct" for the relations of these valuations, for the relation of the authority of values to the authority of active forces) — this historical sense to which we Europeans lay claim as our speciality has come to us in the wake of that enchanting and mad *semi-barbarism* into which Europe had been plunged by the democratic mingling of classes and races: only the nineteenth century knows this sense, as its sixth sense. — Friedrich Nietzsche, *Beyond Good and Evil,* 151.

All philosophers have the common fault that they start from man in his present state and hope to attain their end by an analysis of him. Unconsciously they look upon "man" as an *aeterna veritas*, as a thing unchangeable in all commotion, as a sure standard of things. But everything that the philososopher says about man is really nothing more than testimony about the man of a *very limited* space of time. A lack of the historical sense is the hereditary fault of all philosophers; many, indeed, unconsciously mistake the very latest variety of man, such as has arisen under the influence of certain religions, certain political events, for the permanent form which one must set out. — Nietzsche, *Human, All-Too-Human,* 14, 15.

The word of the past is always an oracle uttered. Only as builders of the future, as knowing the present, will you understand it. — Nietzsche, *Untimely Meditations (Unzeitgemässe Betrachtungen, Werke,* II), 161.

3. Berdyaev writes of history that:

The historic world, or better the historic worlds, which are known from the object, already have to deal with objectivation. The true philosophy of history which is free from objectivation is messianic and prophetic, that is, spiritual. In spiritual knowledge, profoundly existentialist, Truth and Reason are revealed. — Nicolas Berdyaev, *The Real of Spirit and the Realm of Caesar,* 25.

4. Jaspers, whose analysis often appears philosophical in the sense denounced by Nietzsche, nevertheless pays formal attention to the importance of the concept of history in the development of concepts, as is illustrated by the following passage:

Portmann's epoch-making research into the phenomena of man's early childhood and adolescence has revealed, no doubt for the first time, by biological methods, that even as regards his physical structure man achieves his specifically human characteristics with the help of elements pertaining to historical tradition; in other words, man, including his biological traits, cannot be explained merely by the laws of heredity, but must be placed within a historical framework. —Karl Jaspers, *The Perennial Scope of Philosophy*, 56.

5. According to Tillich,

All the Existential philosophers agree on the historical character of immediate personal experience. But the fact that man has a fundamentally "historical Existence" does not mean merely that he has a theoretical interest in the past; his Existence is not directed toward the past at all. It is the attitude not of the detached spectator, but of the actor who must face the future and make personal decisions. — Paul Tillich, *Theology of Culture*, 101.

Tillich's own understanding and use of the concept of history may be seen from the theological perspective in this passage:

It is surprising how casually theological biblicists use a term like "history" when speaking of Christianity as a historical religion or of God as the "Lord of history." They forget that the meaning they connect with the word "history" has been formed by thousands of years of historiography and philosophy of history. They forget that historical being is one kind of being in addition to others and that, in order to distinguish it from the word "nature," for instance, a general vision of the structure of being is presupposed. They forget that the problem of history is tied up with the problems of time, freedom, accident, purpose, etc., and that each of these concepts has had a development similar to the concept of history. The theologian must take seriously the meaning of the terms he uses. They must be known to him in the whole depth and breadth of their meaning. Therefore, the systematic theologian must be a philosopher in critical understanding even if not in creative power. — Tillich, *Systematic Theology*, I, 21.

Life has a dimension which is called "history." And it is helpful to separate the material dealing with the historical aspect of life from the part dealing with life generally. — *Ibid.*, 67.

Historical events, groups, or individuals as such are not mediums of revelation. It is the revelatory constellation into which they enter under special conditions that make them revelatory, not their historical significance or their personal greatness. If history points beyond itself in a correlation of ecstasy and sign-event, revelation occurs. . . . Historical revelation is not revelation *in* history but *through* history. Since man is essentially historical, every revelation, even if it is mediated through a rock or a tree, occurs *in* history. But history itself is revelatory only if a special event or a series of events is experienced ecstatically as miracle. — *Ibid.*, 120.

Without the element of openness, history would be without creativity. It would cease to be history. On the other hand, without that which limits openness, history would be without direction. It would cease to be history. — *Ibid.*, 276.

One of the driving forces behind Tillich's interest in history, besides the interest in theoretical truth, was the tendency of historical research to call into question some facet or other of the Christian revelation, such as the empty tomb at Easter. Thus, Tillich concluded his thinking in this manner:

Theologians need not be afraid of any historical conjecture, for revealed truth lies in a dimension where it can neither be confirmed nor negated by historiography. Therefore, theologians should not prefer some results of historical research to others on theological grounds, and they should not resist results which finally have to be accepted if scientific honesty is not to be destroyed, even if they seem to undermine the knowledge of revelation. Historical investigations should neither comfort nor worry theologians. Knowledge of revelation, although it is mediated primarily through historical events, does not imply factual assertions, and it therefore not exposed to critical analysis by historical research. — *Ibid.*, 130.

6. Heidegger follows Nietzsche in asserting that the historical character of human existence lies in its orientation toward the future. The preoccupation with study of the past is an estrangement from our task as the makers of history. — *Being and Time*, 396.

7. Sartre summarizes concisely the intimate connection between the individual and history by saying:

> Our phenomenological study of the Past, the Present, and the Future allows us to demonstrate that the For-itself can not be except in temporal form. — Jean-Paul Sartre, *Being and Nothingness*, 112.

HOPE:

1. Kierkegaard, in recounting the Abraham story, says that it was necessary for Abraham to have renounced everything, to have given up all hope that things were going to turn out all right in the end, before anything divine could happen to him. Only after having made the infinite resignation, having chosen to go through with the sacrifice of Isaac with no hope of reprieve, could Abraham then receive everything, a substitute sacrifice, and the life of his son and heir.

2. Nietzsche wrote:

> HOPE. — Pandora brought the box of ills and opened it. It was the gift of the gods to men, outwardly a beautiful and seductive gift, and called the Casket of Happiness. Out of it flew all the evils, living winged creatures, thence they now circulate and do men injury day and night. One single evil had not yet escaped from the box, and by the will of Zeus Pandora closed the lid and it remained within. Now for ever man has the casket of happiness in his house and thinks he holds a great treasure; it is at his disposal, he stretches out his hand for it whenever he desires; for he does not know the box which Pandora brought was the casket of evil, and he believes the ill which remains within to be the greatest blessing, — it is hope. Zeus did not wish man, however much he might be tormented by the other evils, to fling away his life, but to go on letting himself be tormented again and again. Therefore he gives man hope, — in reality it is the worst of all evils, because it prolongs the torments of man.
> — Friedrich Nietzsche, *Human, All-Too-Human*, 82.

HUMAN NATURE: There is no settled human nature, according to existentialism. Because the will is more basic than the reason, the choice the individual makes of his own nature is more basic than the rational analysis of that nature.

1. For Kierkegaard there is no truth about human nature which is not the occasion for reflection regarding its validity and source. There is no personal continuity which can be assumed. The only thing there is, is insight, into human subjectivity.

In general, two ways are open for an existing individual to inquire into human nature: *either* he can do his utmost to forget that he is an existing individual, *or* he can concentrate his entire energy upon the fact that he is an existing individual. — *Concluding Unscientific Postscript*, 309.

> The thinker who can forget in all his thinking also to think that he is an existing individual, will never explain life. He merely makes an attempt to cease to be a human being, in order to become a book or an objective something. . . . But it will scarcely be pleasant for him to learn that existence itself mocks everyone who is engaged in becoming purely objective. — *Ibid.*, 85, 86.

2. In Nietzsche's view

> every human being is a unique wonder; they (the artists) dare to show us the human being as he is, down to the last muscle, himself and himself alone — even more, that in this rigorous consistency of his uniqueness he is beautiful and worth contemplating, as novel and incredible as every work of nature, and by no means dull. When a great thinker despises men, it is their laziness that he despises: for it is on account of this that they have the appearance of factory products and seem indifferent and unworthy of companionship or instruction. The human being who does not wish to belong to the mass must merely follow his conscience which shouts at him: "Be yourself! What you are at present doing, thinking, and desiring, that is not

really you." — Nietzsche, *Schopenhauer as Educator,* in Kaufmann, 101, 102.

Nietzsche was agitating for the self-transcendence of man, the overcoming of his present limitation in favor of the new values of the super-man. As preparation for this step, he writes:

> Every enhancement of the type "man" has so far been the work of an aristocratic society — and it will be so again and again — a society that believes in the long ladder of an order of rank and differences in value between man an man, and that needs slavery in some sense or other. Without that *pathos of distance* which grows out of the ingrained difference between strata — when the ruling caste constantly looks afar and looks down upon subjects and instruments and just as constanly practices obedience and command, keeping down and keeping at a distance — that other, more mysterious pathos could not have grown up either — the craving for a never new widening of distances within the soul itself, the development of ever higher, rarer, more remote, furtherstretching, more comprehensive states — in brief, simply the enhancement of the type "man," the continual "self-overcoming of man," to use a moral formula in a supra-moral sense. — Nietzsche, *Beyond Good and Evil,* 201.

This self-transcendence is immoral in the conventional sense, being similar as it is to the barbarian circumstances from which strong cultures took their rise. In the light of this lust for power, this unbroken dominance of the will which produced aristocratic societies, the super-man will take his rise.

> Man is a rope stretched between the animal and the Super-man — a rope over an abyss.
> A dangerous crossing, a dangerous wayfaring, a dangerous looking-back, a dangerous trembling and halting.
> What is great in man is that he is a bridge and not a goal: what is lovable in man is that he is an *over-going* and a *down-going.*

I love those that know not how to live except as down-goers, for they are the over-goers.

I love the great despisers, because they are the great adorers, and arrows of longing for the other shore.

I love the great despisers, because they are the great stars for going down and being sacrifices, but sacrifice themselves to the earth, that the earth of the Superman may hereafter arrive. — Nietzsche, *Thus Spake Zarathustra,* 8, 9.

3. Berdyaev, commenting on the theories of the nineteenth century in general and Nietzsche in particular, writes that

A new man, something new within man, predicates that man continues to exist, in his human quality. No alternation, no matter how important, can make a man out of an ape. The Nietzschean idea of the superman is a yearning for something higher, but it is betrayal of man and of humanity. This is talk of the rise of a new kind, a new race, divine, diabolic, or just animal. But not of the new man. The new man is connected with the eternal man, with the eternal in man. — Nicolas Berdyaev, *The Realm of Spirit and the Realm of Caesar,* 163.

4. Jaspers writes that:

Man is an object of inquiry for anatomy, physiology, psychology and sociology. Anthropology — ethnology and morphology — studies his physical existence as a whole. We have acquired a considerable body of knowledge, the basic feature of which is that all its insights, even the relative generalizations, are particular; the insights remain scattered, do not combine into a complete system. Consequently this knowledge of man always goes astray when it leads to total judgments on man, to supposed understanding of the whole. — Karl Jaspers, *The Perennial Scope of Philosophy,* 54.

Pain is the birthplace of the man who has a will to history. Only the man who exposes his soul to evil fortune can learn what things are like and be stimulated to change them. The condition for the birth of his concrete freedom is that he does not shut himself off, does not blindly let himself be destroyed or wait still things are past and then live as though they had not been. — Jaspers, *The European Spirit,* 40.

5. Tillich surveys the general attitude of existential thought toward the question of human nature, dissenting from its theoretical basis, particularly as formulated by Sartre.

One must ask: What is this self that affirms itself? Radical Existentialism answers: What it makes of itself. This is all it can say, because anything more would restrict the absolute freedom of the self. The self, cut off from participation in its world, is an empty shell, a mere possibility. It must act because it lives, but it must redo every action because acting involves him who acts in that upon which he acts. It gives content and for this reason it restrics his freedom to make of himself what he wants. In classical theology, both Catholic and Protestant, only God has this prerogative: He is *ā sē* (from himself) or absolute freedom. Nothing is in him which is not by him. Existentialism, on the basis of the message that God is dead, gives man the divine "a-se-ity." Nothing shall be in man which is not by man. But man is finite, he is given to himself as what he is. He has received his being and with it the structure of his being, including the structue of finite freedom. And finite freedom is not aseity. Man can affirm himself only if he affirms not an empty shell, a mere possibility, but the structure of being in which he finds himself before action and nonaction. Finite freedom has a definite structure, and if the self tries to trespass on this structure it ends in the loss of itself. The nonparticipating hero in Sartre's *The Age of Reason* is caught in a net of contingencies, coming partly from the subconscious levels of his own self, partly from the environment from which he cannot withdraw. The assuredly empty self is filled with contents which enslave it just because it does not know or accept them as contents. This is true too of the cynic, as was said before. He cannot escape the forces of his self which may drive him into complete loss of the freedom that he wants to preserve. — Paul Tillich, *The Courage to be,* 151, 152.

6. According to Heidegger, it is impossible to approach Being through objective reality. "Existential Being," Dasein *(q.v.)*, or self-relatedness is the only door to Being itself. The objective world, which he calls *Das Vorhandene,* is a late and derivative product of immediate personal experience.

7. Sartre writes of "human-reality," or, in his more technical terminology, of the "For-itself." It is used both generally, as an equivalent for mankind as well as for the individual man. In considering the relationship between the subjective and the objective world, Sartre takes the body as a prime subject.

If then we wish to reflect on the nature of the body, it is necessary to establish an order of our reflections which conforms to the order of being: we can not continue to confuse the ontological levels, and we must in succession examine the body first as being-for-itself and then as being-for-others. And in order to avoid such absurdities as "inverted vision," we must keep constantly in mind the idea that since these two aspects of the body are on different and incommunicable levels of being, they can not be reduced to one another. Being-for-itself must be wholly body and it must be wholly consciousness; it can not be *united* with a body. Similarly being-for-others is wholly body; there are no "psychic phenomena" there to be united with the body. There is nothing *behind the body.* But the body is wholly "psychic." — Jean-Paul Sartre, *Being and Nothingness,* 281.

See Also: Man; Existence; Subjectivity.

I

IDEAL: An important concept for Kierkegaard's later thought. As he sought to apply his concepts to social and religious conditions, he made extensive use of the category of the ideal. Not defined, it was considered a self-evident idea, the ideal being contrasted with the actual.

1. According to Kierkegaard,

The ideal means hatred of man. What man naturally loves is finitude. To face him with the ideal is the most dreadful torture. Certainly, when the ideal is produced in the most exalted poetic fashion, like an enchanting vision of the imagination, he accepts this pleasure.

But when the ideal is produced as the ethico-religious demand, it is the most dreadful torture of man. . . . — Søren Kierkegaard, *The Last Years*, 308, 309.

2. Jaspers rejects the value of ideals, as he explains in the following passage:

Conscious of his freedom, man desires to become what he can and should be. He conceives an *ideal* of his nature. As on the plane of cognition, the idea of man as an object of scientific inquiry may lead to a falsely definitive image of him, so on the plane of freedom he may falsely choose a path leading to an absolute ideal. From helpless questioning and bewilderment, he thus aspires to take refuge in a universal that he can imitate in its concrete forms.

There are numerous images of man that have served as ideals with which we wished to identify ourselves. There is no doubt that such ideals have been effective, and that social types actually influence our behavior. The ideal can be magnified to a vague conception of man's "greatness," of something in man that is in a sense more than human, that is superhuman or inhuman. . . .

Just as we lose sight of man when he becomes an object of scientific inquiry in racial theory, psychoanalysis, or Marxism and is represented as fully understandable, so we lose sight of the human task when he becomes an ideal. — Karl Jaspers, *The Perennial Scope of Philosophy*, 67, 68.

All ideals of man are impossible, because man's potentialities are infinite. There can be no perfect man. This has important philosophical consequences.

1. The true value of man lies, not in the species or type that he approximates, but in the historical individual, for whom no substitution or replacement is possible. — *Ibid.*, 69.

See Also: Good.

IMMORTALITY:
This topic, of tremendous interest to the history of western philosophy in general, is of little interest to Existentialism. Except for its similarity to the concept of eternity *(c.f.* Eternal Recurrence), only these Existential thinkers whose orientation is more traditional discuss the topic. Most Existentialists prefer to discuss and analyze the present and the immediate future rather than the transcendent reality of a supernatural worldview.

1. Berdyaev writes, sympathetically, that

Eternal life is revealed in time, it may unfold itself in every instant as an eternal present. Eternal life is not a future life but life in the present, life in the depths of an instant of time. In those depths time is torn asunder. It is therefore a mistake to expect eternity in the future, in an existence beyond the grave and to look forward to death in time in order to enter in to the divine eternal life. Strictly speaking, eternity will never come in the future — in the future there can only be a bad infinity. Only hell can be thought of in this way. Eternity and eternal life come not in the future but in a moment, i.e. they are a deliverance from time, and mean ceasing to project life into time. — Nicolas Berdyaev, *The Destiny of Man,* 262.

Eternal and immortal life is possible for man not because it is natural to the human soul, but because Christ rose from the dead and conquered the deadly powers of the world — because in the cosmic miracle of the Resurrection meaning has triumphed over meaninglessness. — Berdyaev, *The Destiny of Man,* 258.

Turning from these ideas to the critical basis which he believes to ground them in modern thought, Berdyaev states:

The philosophical idea of the natural immortality of the soul deduced from its substantiality leads nowhere. It ignores the fact of death and denies the tragedy of it. — *Ibid.,* 254.

Natural immortality belongs to the species or to the race but not to the individual. Immortality has to be won by the person and involves struggle for personality. — *Ibid.,* 255.

2. Jaspers, writing from a slightly different critical position, states:

Immortality, however, means eternity, in which past and future are canceled. Though the moment is temporal, it nevertheless participates, when fulfilled existentially, in time-trascending eternity. The "eternity of the moment" is a self-contradicting thought. It seeks to express the truth, in which the reality of temporal embodiment is one with timeless ideality of Being: as the eternality of the Real. — Karl Jaspers, *Philosophy Is for Everyman,* 111.

We are mortal as mere empirical beings, immortal when we appear in time as that which is eternal. We are mortal when we are loveless, immortal as lovers. We are mortal in indecision, immortal in resolution. We are mortal as natural processes, immortal when given to ourselves in freedom. — *Ibid.,* 112.

3. Tillich, similarly, writes:

Christianity must reject the doctrine of natural immortality and must affirm instead the doctrine of eternal life given by God as the power of being-itself. — Paul Tillich, *Systematic Theology*, I, 188.

The question of the unchangeable in our being, like the question of the unchangeable in being-itself, is an expressions of the anxiety of losing substance and identity. To dismiss this question with the correct assertion that the arguments for the so-called immortality of the soul are wrong, that they are attempts to escape the seriousness of the question of substantiality by establishing an endless continuation of what is essentially finite, is unjustified. The question of unchangeable substance cannot be silenced. It expresses the anxiety implied in the always threatening loss of substance, that is, of identity with one's self and the power of maintaining one's self. —*Ibid.*, 198.

It will be noted that the argument in the preceding paragraph, that the question of permanence must be taken seriously, rests upon the existential proposition, that the deep emotions (such as anxiety) are of a necessary character in the consideration of theoretical questions.

Tillich did not believe in life after death, nor did he believe that it mattered except to those who had very recently lost someone close to them, and even to them, only for a short while.

INDIVIDUAL: One of the key Existential themes, originating with Kierkegaard, expressing the opposition to idealism, to any tyranny whether rational or legal over the right of the existing person to choose the course and nature of his own life.

1. Kierkegaard's philosophical thought was aimed at helping men to see their existential situation, to understand the alternatives facing them, and to choose, to commit themselves, to

become "existing individuals." Kierkegaard strongly opposes the modern tendency to submerge the individual in collectivity, "the mob." Kierkegaard always gave a religious significance to the concept of existence. This religious setting is retained, to a large extent, by Karl Jaspers. With Sartre, the Kierkegaardian themes, authentic existence, free self-commitment, and dread are divorced from their original religious setting and employed in an atheistic frame of reference.

In Kierkegaard's interpretation of the transition from essence to existence, in *The Concept of Dread,* he declares that the *dread* of finitude drives man to action. At the same time, it drives man to an alienation from his essential being to the more profound *dread* of guilt and despair.

> The Individual is the category through which . . . this age, all history, and the human race as a whole, must pass. — Søren Kierkegaard, *The Point of View for My Work as an Author.*

2. Nietzsche has somewhat the same thought, but with a different term. He calls the Individual "The Free Spirit." The Free Spirits are those who understand and respond to Nietzsche's philosophy, those who are not bound by convention and moral customs, those willing to be free from constraints to face the future with courage and confidence, ready for the advent of new values and the production of the super-man.

3. In Jaspers' conception,

> The individual is opposed to universal laws, norms, necessities; untragically, he represents mere willfulness opposing the law; tragically, he represents the genuine exception which, though opposing the law, yet has truth on his side.
>
> General principles are concentrated in the forces of society, social stratification, rules, and offices. Hence society may give rise to tragedy. On the other hand, general principles may be concentrated in human character as an imperative of eternal laws which run counter to the drives and the personality of the individual. Hence there are also tragedies that arise from character. — Karl Jaspers, *Tragedy Is Not Enough,* 47, 48.

According to Jaspers, every personal Existence is unique. "We are completely irreplaceable. We are not merely cases of universal Being." — Jaspers, *Reason and Existenz,* 19.

4. Tillich writes that

The very term "individual" points to the interdependence of self-relatedness and individualization. A self-centered being cannot be divided. It can be destroyed, or it can be deprived of certain parts out of which new self-centered beings emerge. . . . Man not only is completely self-centered: he also is completely individualized. — Paul Tillich, *Systematic Theology,* I, 175.

5. Heidegger speaks of the *Jemeinigkeit* of existence, meaning that it belongs to me and nobody else. When men are in social contact with each other, they generally cover over their real inner personal experience with talk and activity. But the individual in his inner loneliness experiences conscience, guilt, and the prospect of death.

6. In Sartre's essay on Existentialism, he writes:
The first effect of existentialism is that it puts every man in possession of himself as he is, and places the entire responsibility for his existence squarely upon his on shoulders. — Jean-Paul Sartre, *Existentialism is a Humanism,* in Kaufmann. 291,

IN-ITSELF: (French *en-soi*) Sartre's term for non-conscious reality, as contrasted with conscious reality, or the being of the human person (being-for-itself, *q.v.*). Sartre distinguishes three modes of being: (1) being-in-itself, (2) being-for-itself, and (3) being-for-others.

The "in-itself" is the being which rests in itself and exists independently of us; it is the being of such things as tables.

See Also: Being-for-itself; Being-for-others.

J

JASPERS, KARL (1883-1969). One of the five most important existential philosophers (with Kierkegaard, Nietzsche, Heidegger, and Sartre), Karl Jaspers was born on February 23, 1883, at Oldenburg, in Germany, near the North Sea coast. His father was the sheriff of the district, later to be a director of the bank.

Karl studied law at the universities of Heidelberg and Munich. After three semesters he changed his course of study to medicine. By 1909 he became an M. D. Serving as a voluntary assistant at the psychiatric hospital of the University of Heidelberg, he became *Privatdocent* on the psychological faculty in 1913.

In 1914 "the World War caused the great breach in our European existence." His interests changed, and he began teaching philosophy. After five years, he was appointed professor of philosophy, in 1921.

His first two attempts at a systematic work were the *General Psychopathology* in 1913 and the *Psychology of the World-View* in 1919. These were followed by *Philosophy,* 1932. In this work, Jaspers seeks to illuminate existence by facing objective thought on one side and transcendence on the other. The problem is how to conceive existence without making it into an objective thing, on the one hand, and without lapsing into irrationality or poetry or silence on the other. Existence as embodied is the human condition revealed in such "limiting situations" as suffering, death, guilt, struggle, being tied to a body and to a world-view. Existence in this first sense is to live in a situation which we did not choose, but which is not alien. Existence in the second sense, as selective, implies freedom to choose. In this sense we are responsible for ourselves. Although an authentic choice is not arbitrary, neither can it be completely reduced to a rational argument. We both choose what we are and we choose from the nature of what we are. Existence in the third sense, as communicating, implies communication between existents by language or some other means. There is no absolute perspective that embraces all points of view. Nevertheless, no one is confined only to his own point of view. Each perspective is to some extent available to everyone. Thus, as the effort of one to transcend his own limited perspective, this communication leads to truth.

In 1937, Jaspers was dismissed from his teaching position for political reasons by the National Socialist government.

Not until 1945 was he reinstated in office with the consent of the American occupation authorities. In 1948 he was appointed professor of philosophy at Basel, the university where Nietzsche had taught.

His later works include *Von der Wahrheit*, 1948, *Vom Ursprung und Ziel der Geschichte*, 1949, and *Einführung in die Philosophie*, 1950.

On February 26, 1969, Karl Jaspers died with his wife, Gertrud, at his bedside.

K

KIERKEGAARD, SOREN AABYE (1813-1855): The founder of of the philosophy of existence, this Danish thinker was born in Copenhagen ("Market-harbor") on May 5, 1813. He lived a parochial life, never travelling farther from his home town than Berlin, and that for only a few months.

He also lived a bourgeois life in the classic sense. His father Michael, a West Jutland shepherd who had moved to Copenhagen and made a fortune as a wool merchant, left Søren a large inheritance so that his son did not have to work.

The first stage in Søren's life can be said to be the years up to 1838, when his father died. The second was the period of his authorship, a time of phenomenal literary production, during which he wrote no less than thirty books. The third stage, beginning in 1854, was the time of his attack on the state church, the beginning of the direct application of his theories to the institutions of his day. This third stage was cut short by his death within a year, a type of martyrdom or sacrifice, at the age of 42.

The first stage in his life (1813-1838) was dominated by the personality of his father. In his early youth, Michael had cursed God for his lonely, cold, bitter, and hungry life tending sheep on the barren Jutland heath. Soon after this, he was given his first opportunity to enter the world of business. Prospering beyond his wildest dreams, Michael believed that his success was a kind of perverse judgment upon him. God was showering him with undeserved blessings. Wealthy enough to retire from active business in his forties, Michael devoted his energies and finances to making high friends in the church. Yet, try as he may, he could never escape the uneasy feeling that he was doomed for his sin. His family would suffer for his transgression.

A secondary cause of the old man's guilt was sexual. His wife had died. Before the period of prescribed mourning was over, he slept with the household maid. He then married her, but he could never forgive her — or himself — for this incident.

The idea grew that he would be punished by having his family's name blotted out from the earth. None of his children would outlive the father. As Søren wrote:

> I suspected that my father's ripe old age was not a divine blessing, but rather a curse; that our family's excellent mental gifts served only to excite us mutually; I felt the stillness of death rise around me when in my father I saw a doomed man destined to survive us all, a cross on the grave of his own hopes. A guilt must be weighing on our entire family; God's punishment must be upon it; our family was to vanish, swept aside by God's mighty hand, blotted out, erased like an experiment gone wrong. . . . —
> Søren Kierkegaard, *The Diary of Søren Kierkegaard*, 30, 31.

There was sufficient reason to suppose that this might be the case. Beginning in 1819 the first of the seven children of the family died, Michael, aged twelve. Two and a half years later his sister, Maren, died, aged twenty-four. In 1832 Nicolene died at the age of thirty-three. In the next year Niels died in the USA. Only one year later the last sister died, together with Søren's mother. The only surviving children were Søren and his older brother, Peter.

Therefore, when his father died at the age of eighty-three, Søren was amazed to have outlived him. The family curse had been proven wrong. One of the most striking indications of Søren's state of mind at this turn of events is the title of his first published work: *From the Papers of One Still Living.*

The second stage in his life thus began in 1838. He was freed by the death of his father to live his own life. He became engaged to be married in 1840 to Regina Olsen. However, he felt that he could not be completely honest with her about his "secret," and, in the light of this difficulty, broke off the engagement by pretending to have been merely toying with her affections.

110

Instead of devoting himself to marriage, he devoted himself to writing. His "secret" was somehow connected with his authorship in a way which has not been satisfactorily explained by any of the commentators.

It goes without saying that I cannot explain my work as an author wholly, i.e. with the purely personal inwardness in which I possess the explanation of it. And this in part because I cannot make public my God-relationship . . . in part because I cannot wish (and no one can desire that I might) to obtrude upon anyone what concerns only my private person — though naturally there is much in this which for me serves to explain my work as an author. — Søren Kierkegaard, *The Point of View for My Work as an Author*: *A Report to History*, 9.

Kierkegaard meant to conceal the driving force which simultaneously prevented him from marrying and drove him to writing:

After my death no one will find among my papers a single explanation as to what really filled my life (that is my consolation); no one will find the words which explain everything and which often made what the world would call a trifle into an event of tremendous importance to me, and what I look upon as something insignificant when I take away the secret gloss which explains all. — Kierkegaard, *Journal*, 85.

The most common theories about this secret are (1) that he did not want to tell Regina that his father had cursed God as a young man, (2) that he did not want to reveal his father's indiscretions with the maid, (3) that he had visited a brothel on a drunken spree with some friends — this theory is contradicted by the *Diary* when one of the three things for which he thanks God is "that no living being owes existence to me", (4) that his uncle was confined in a mental hospital for sexual maladjustment, which in those days meant the crime of masturbation.

The only certain result of the foregoing speculation is that

Kierkegaard chose to write in pseudonyms, a fact which indicates the central importance he attached to the art of concealment, a facet of his work which ranks equal with his skill at communicating — dialectically. He was careful, in Copenhagen, to hide his serious work as an author behind a mask of frivolity. He took a break from his writing just at the time of the intermission at the theater so that he could mingle with the theater-goers, who were convinced that he was living the life of a wealthy playboy.

His books, surveyed in chronological order, are (1) *From the Papers of One Still Living,* published "against his will by S. Kierkegaard," a book critical of Hans Christian Andersen's poor novel, (2) *The Concept of Irony,* the dissertation for his Master's Degree from the University, where he had enrolled as a theology student (1841), (3) *Either/Or* (1843), (4) *Eighteen Edifying Discourses* (1843, 1844, 1845), (5) *Repetition,* by Constantine Constantius (1843), initially discusses the happiness that man has lost, saying that such happiness cannot be repeated by revisiting happy places, because it is the man himself who has changed, (6) *Fear and Trembling,* by Johannes de Silentio, (1843) which declares that man's plight is only within himself, and that communication is only possible through silence, (7) *Philosophical Fragments,* by Johannes Climacus, (1844) whose theme is the truth which educates, that man does not need a new philosophy but a new authentic self, a self that can be discovered in the encounter with God, an encounter which is a paradox that forces man to go beyond reason for the answers to his deepest questions, (8) *The Concept of Dread,* by The Watchman of Copenhagen, Vigilius Haufniensis, (1844) which investigates the psychological relation between dread and sin, concluding that the nature of man's *self* is freedom, an existential theme to be repeated by many other existential thinkers, (9) The book of *Prefaces,* by Nicolaus Notabene, (1844) was a frivolous book intended to do nothing more than re-convince the Copenhagen public that the writer remained a dandy lacking any seriousness, (10) *Three Discourses on Imagined Occasions,* by S. Kierkegaard, imagines useful remarks for the occasions of confession, marriage, and graveside, (11) *Stages on Life's Way,* edited by Hilarius Bookbinder and written by seven other authors, (1845), (12) The

Concluding Unscientific Postcript to the Philosophical Fragments,
by Johannes Climacus with S. Kierkegaard as publisher, sum-
marizing the whole project of thought to date, The big *Book on
Adler,* here unnumbered because it was written by Kierkegaard
but never published, discusses in detail the case of a teacher who
was fired by the authorities because he claimed to have had a
direct revelation from God, (13) *A Literary Review,* by Kierkegaard, (1846) is a kind of interlude from philosophical thought,
being more a critical review of the novel *Two Ages,* the age of
antiquity which was characterized by leadership, the age of Christendom which was characterized by representation, and the present age which is characterized by the drive for equality, (14)
Edifying Discourses in Various Spirits, by Kierkegaard, (1847)
says, first, that purity of heart means to will one thing, second,
that important things may be learned from the contemplation of
the lillies of the field, and third, that there is a gospel of suffering, (15) *The Works of Love,* (1847) develops a theory of
social ethics on religious grounds, (16) *Christian Discourses,*
(1848) states that true Christianity needs no rational defence, nor
is its cause served by any such apology, (17) *The Crisis and A
Crisis in the Life of an Actress,* by Inter et inter, "Among and
Between," (1848), (18) *Lillies of the Field and the Birds of the
Air,* (1849), (19) *Two Minor Ethico-Religious Treatises,* by
"H. H.", (1849) is really not so minor, containing as it does the
distinction between a genius and an apostle, and asking whether
a man has the right to let himself be put to death on behalf of
the truth, (20) *The Sickness Unto Death,* by Anti-Climacus, which
explains that the frustration of the inner self is really a sickness,
one which can be cured by God, but if not, then the sickness becomes sin, (21) *High-Priest — The Publican — The Woman That
Was a Sinner,* (1849), (22) *The Point of View for My Work as
an Author,* by Kierkegaard, (written in 1848 but not published
until 1859, four years posthumously) explains the three phases
of what he called his "authorship" in the technical sense, and
states that he himself in all those stages was the religious author,
(23) *About My Work as an Author,* (1849) provides another
explanation of his authorship, to the confusion of scholars, (24)
Training in Christianity, by Anti-Climacus, "edited by S. Kierke-

113

gaard," (25) *An Up-Building Discourse,* (1850), (26) *Two Talks at the Communion on Fridays,* (1851), (27) *For Self-Examination,* (1851), (28) *Judge for Yourself!,* (1851), (29) The collected newspaper articles up to the year 1854, (30) The newspaper articles from 1854 to 1855, (31) *The Instant* pamphlets taken collectively, pamphlets agitating against the established church, (32) *What Christ's Judgment Is Upon Official Christianity,* (1855) and *God's Unchangeableness.*

Kierkegaard also uses the term "authorship" in a technical sense to classify his writings by their subject-matter. Although this classification of his does not account for all his writings, it is useful to know what he did include in this way. He divides his "authorship" into three groups: esthetic, transitional, and purely religious. The first group, esthetic, consists of seven books: *Either/ Or, Fear and Trembling, Repetition, The Concept of Dread, Prefaces, Philosophical Fragments,* and *Stages on Life's Way,* together with eighteen of the edifying discourses. The second group, transitional, consists of only one work, the *Concluding Unscientific Postcript.* The third group, purely religious works, contains three major works: *Edifying Discourses in Various Spirits, The Works of Love,* and *Christian Discourses,* "along with," Kierkegaard adds, "a little esthetic article, *The Crisis and A Crisis in the Life of an Actress.*"

The third stage in Kierkegaard's life began in 1854, on the 18th of December, which was when he began his attack on the Danish State Church by the publication of his letter in the *Fatherland,* a conservative newspaper, the *Wall Street Journal* of the time. Gone was his elaborate method of indirect communication. He wrote directly on the issues of the day. He applied his principles forcefully and deliberately to the ills of his time.

The essential continuity of this stage with his previous literary production is illustrated by the following passage:

> The contents of this little book affirm, then, what I truly am as an author, that I am and was a religious author, that the whole of my work as an author is related to Christianity, to the problem "of becoming a Christian," with a direct or indirect polemic against the monstrous illusion we call Christendom, or against the illusion that in such a land as ours

all are Christians of a sort. — Kierkegaard, *The Point of View for My Work as an Author: A Report to History, 5, 6.*

The distinguishing feature of this third stage is that it, like the second, is marked by a death. In this case it was the death of Bishop Mynster, his father's close friend and the family pastor. Bishop Mynster's death released Kierkegaard from his silence about the state of the church, about its departure from the nature and requirements of true Christian Faith.

Professor Martensen preached the funeral oration for Bishop Mynster, and in the eulogy far exceeded the bounds of what was appropriate, in Kierkegaard's view. Martensen praised Mynster, calling him "a genuine witness for the Truth," a witness "not only in word and profession, but in deed and in truth," truly a member of "the holy chain of witnesses which stretches from the days of the apostles."

Professor Martensen's praise was not entirely disinterested, for he himself hoped to be elected as the Bishop's successor. This situation was the signal for Kierkegaard to begin his attack. He did not allow his articles to be used as ammunition in the political battle for the succession to the bishopric, withholding publication until that issue was decided.

Bishop Mynster had been both a wise administrator and a distinguished preacher. He had a deep sense of devotional piety and pastoral concern for his people. His strength was his failing, in Kierkegaard's judgment. That is, Mynster had confused counseling with witnessing. Mild, practical pastoral advice is not identical with authentic Christianity. Giving advice is not the same as giving your life. A counselor is not a martyr.

Kierkegaard carried on his attack against the church's compromises with great energy. In the midst of the growing public controversy, Kierkegaard died, on the fourth of November, 1855. He was buried one week later, his funeral the site of a near riot between his supporters and the defenders of the established church.

In English, the most influential of Kierkegaard's works has been the *Attack Upon 'Christendom'*, which was the beginning of his direct application of his ideas to social issues and institutions. Next after this have been his "esthetic" works, especially the *Philosophical Fragments, Either/Or, and Fear* and *Trembling.*

The "transitional" book, *Concluding Unscientific Postcript,* has also had its impact upon the English-speaking world. Of least influence have been his "purely religious" books.

The one concept which has had the most profound influence upon philosophy as a whole has been the idea that an existential "system" is impossible. That is, a body of necessary knowledge that deals with experience is not possible. The reason for this assertion is that we are not capable of discovering necessary truths about historical, changing events. This is the key concept in existential thinking, one which has been repeated and expanded by the existentialists who were to follow.

KNOWLEDGE:

1. For Kierkegaard, the term knowledge was ambiguous. If it meant the Hegelian attempt to understand the world and man in completely rational terms, then it represented the idealistic system which Existential thinking completely opposed.

If knowledge meant knowing in an Existential sense, then it stood for somewhat the same concept as subjectivity (*q.v.*). In this sense the major term would be subjectivity, while the minor term would be knowledge.

The most notable use Kierkegaard makes of the term is in the first sense, the Hegelian notion, as in the following quotation:

Knowledge demolishes Jesus Christ. — Søren Kierkegaard, *Training in Christianity,* 36.

This means the same as:

From history one can learn nothing about Christ. — *Ibid.,* 28.

That is, Kierkegaard believed that it is impossible to base faith upon knowledge, especially knowledge about historical events. Knowledge cannot provide certainty, not for the existing individual, and it is a fatal distraction for the individual to attempt to ground his faith in knowledge. It is impossible in any case, and it diverts his attention from his primary task, which is choosing authentic existence.

2. Nietzsche warns against any effort to identify Being or

116

Reality with the objects of thought. Any such identification is the great threat to personal human Existence in our time.

Knowledge and Becoming exclude each other. Consequently knowledge must signify something different. A "will to make recognizable" must precede it; a special kind of becoming, man, must have created the deception of Being. — Friedrich Nietzsche, *Will to Power,* 387.

Origin of Knowledge. — Throughout immense stretches of time the intellect produced nothing but errors; some of them proved to be useful and preservative of the species: he who fell in with them, or inherited them, waged the battle for himself and his offspring with better success. Those erroneous articles of faith which were successively transmitted by inheritance, and have finally become almost the property and stock of the human species, are, for example, the following: — that there are enduring things, that there are equal things, that there are things, substances, and bodies, that a thing is what it appears, that our will is free, that what is good for me is also good absolutely. It was only very late that the deniers and doubters of such propositions came forward, — it was only very late that truth made its appearance as the most impotent form of knowledge. — Nietzsche, *The Joyful Wisdom, III,* 153, 154.

As proof of his contention that truth is not a useful concept for the advancement of man, Nietzsche appeals to biology:

It seemed as if it were impossible to get along with truth, our organism was adapted for the very opposite; all its higher functions, the perceptions of the senses, and in general every kind of sensation, co-operated with those primevally embodied, fundamental errors. — *Ibid.,* 154.

Nietzsche blames philosophy for timidity in concentrating on epistemology to the exclusion of the broader areas of speculative thought:

Philosophy reduced to "theory of knowledge," in fact no more than a timid epochism and doctrine of abstinence — a philosophy that never gets beyond the threshold and takes pains to *deny* itself the right to enter — that is philosophy in its last throes, an end, an agony, something inspiring pity. How could such a philosophy — *dominate!* — Nietzsche, *Beyond Good and Evil*, 123.

3. Berdyaev writes that

Man . . . lost the power of knowing real being . . . lost access to reality and (was) reduced to studying knowledge. One cannot arrive at being — one can only start with it. — Nicolas Berdyaev, *Solitude and Society*.

4. According to Jaspers,

The will utilizes these possibilities in knowledge to its own advantage. A battle arises for and against reason. Opposed to pure, transparent reason's drive toward rest within the conceivable, stands a drive to destroy reason, not only to indicate its limits, but to enslave it. We want to subordinate ourselves to an inconceivable supersensible, which however appears in the world through human utterances and makes demands. We wish to subordinate ourselves to the natural character of impulses and passions, to the immediacy of what is now present. These drives are now translated by the philosophy which adheres to them into a knowledge of the non-rational: philosophy expresses its falling into the non-rational, the counter-rational, and the super-rational as a knowledge about them. Yet, even in the most radical defiance of reason, there remains a minimum of rationality. — Karl Jaspers, *Kierkegaard and Nietzsche*, in Kaufmann, 159.

5. Tillich, in his initial discussion of theology, writes:

Theology claims that it constitutes a special realm of knowledge, that it deals with a special object and employs a special method. This claim places the theologian under the obligation of giving an account of the way in which he relates theology to other forms of knowledge. — Paul Tillich, *Systematic Theology*, I, 18.

In the course of his work, Tillich makes the following assertions about knowledge:

Knowing is a form of union. In every act of knowledge the knower and that which is known are united; the gap between subject and object is overcome. The subject "grasps" the object, adapts it to itself, and, at the same time, adapts itself to the object. But the union of knowledge is a peculiar one; it is a union through separation. Detachment is the condition of cognitive union. In order to know, one must "look" at a thing, and, in order to look at a thing, one must be "at a distance." — *Ibid.,* 94.

The element of union and the element of detachment appear in different proportions in the different realms of knowledge. But there is no knowledge without the presence of both elements. . . . The type of knowledge which is predominantly determined by the element of detachment can be called "controlling knowledge." Controlling knowledge is the outstanding, though not the only, example of technical reason. It unites subject and object for the sake of the control of the object by the subject. — *Ibid.,* 97.

But this is neither the way of knowing human nature nor is it the way of knowing any individual personality in past or present, including one's self. Without union there is no cognitive approach to man. In contrast to controlling knowledge this cognitive attitude can be called "receiving knowledge". Neither actually no potentially is it determined by the means-ends relationship. Receiving knowledge takes the object into itself, into union with the subject. This includes the emotional element, from which controlling knowledge tries to detach itself as much as possible. — *Ibid.,* 98.

Existentialism tries to save the freedom of the individual self from the domination of controlling knowledge. But this freedom is described in terms which not only lack any criterion but also any content. Existentialism is the most desperate attempt to escape the power of controlling knowledge and of the objectified world which technical reason has produced. It says

119

"No" to this world, but, in order to say "Yes" to something else, it has either to use controlling knowledge or to turn to revelation. — *Ibid.,* 100.

Knowledge stands in a dilemma; controlling knowledge is safe but not ultimately significant, while receiving knowledge can be ultimately significant, but it cannot give certainty. — *Ibid.,* 105.

6. Sartre writes of the relation of knowledge to the individual in these terms:

We shall grant to idealism that the being of the For-itself is knowledge of being, but we must add that this knowledge has being. The identity of the being of the For-itself and of knowledge does not come from the fact that knowledge is the measure of being but from the fact that the For-itself makes known to itself what it is, through the in-itself; that is, from the fact that in its being it is a relation to being. — Jean-Paul Sartre, *Being and Nothingness,* 192.

To realism, on the other hand, we shall grant that it is being which is present to consciousness in knowledge and that the For-itself adds *nothing* to the In-itself except the very fact that *there* is In-itself; that it, the affirmative negation. — *Ibid.,* 193.

Knowledge puts us in the presence of the absolute, and there is a truth of knowledge. But this truth, although releasing to us nothing more and nothing less than the absolute, remains strictly human. — *Ibid.,* 194.

See also: Subjectivity.

L

LAW: (attribution uncertain, but akin to Old Norman *lag,* due place, layer; and to Old High German, ur*lag,* fate)

Every law is a tyranny over the living man. As an objective and universal thing, law seeks to control the individual and impair his freedom. The particular view taken of law by the various Existential thinkers will depend on their view of the more general term, "good" (*q.v.*).

1. Kierkegaard thought that the law was irrelevant to the inward life of the individual. The life of choice was not dependent upon such activities as trying to reform the laws of the land, and Kierkegaard took no part in the legal reforms being debated and enacted in the Denmark of his day, changes as far-reaching as changing from an absolute monarchy to a limited (constitutional) monarchy.

The primary relation of the individual was not to the universal (the law, the ethical sphere) but to the absolute (God, the religious sphere).

2. Nietzsche writes:

Arbitrary Law Necessary. — . . . With us, law is no longer custom, it can only *command* and be compulsion; none of us any longer possesses a traditional sense of justice; we must therefore content ourselves with *arbitrary laws,* which are the expressions of the necessity that there *must be* law. The most logical is then in any case the most acceptable, because it is the most *impartial,* granting even that in every case the smallest unit of measure in the relation of crime and punishment is arbitrarily fixed. — Friedrich Nietzsche, *Human, All-Too-Human,* 331, 332.

121

3. Tillich approaches the topic of law by making a distinction:

> With this insight into the two different meanings of law, law as structure and law as the demand to actualize this structure, we approach the question: has the law in the second sense a motivating power for the fulfillment of the moral imperative and its concrete demands? — Paul Tillich, *Morality and Beyond,* 49.

> The general question is: can the commanding law, which presupposes the contrast between our essential and our actual being, motivate us to transform ourselves in the direction of reuniting the actual with the essential? The first logically consistent answer: it *cannot!* For the very existence of the commanding law is based on that split. — *Ibid.*

Following a detailed and discursive analysis of the topic, Tillich also adds

> The law provides moral motivation if morality becomes a thread within a texture of premoral forces and motives. — *Ibid.,* 56.

4. Frankl, the Existential psychologist, tells this incident about the operation of the concept of law within a concentration camp:

> It had been a bad day. On parade, an announcement had been made about the many actions that would, from then on, be regarded as sabotage and therefore punishable by immediate death by hanging. Among these were crimes such as cutting small strips from our old blankets (in order to improvise ankle supports) and very minor "thefts." A few days previously a semi-starved prisoner had broken into the potato store to steal a few pounds of potatoes. The theft had been discovered and some prisoners had recognized the "burglar." When the camp authorities heard about it they ordered that the guilty man be given up to them or the whole camp would starve for a day. Naturally the 2,500 men preferred to fast. — Viktor Frankl, *From Death Camp to Existentialism,* 102.

See also: Good.

LOGOTHERAPY: In Existential psychology, the term for Dr. Viktor Frank's therapy. The theory states that the spiritual aspects of the distressed individuals require treatment rather than the physical symptoms. Thus it is named Logotherapy, from the Greek word, "logos," which is "word," "meaning," or "spiritual."

"Logos" being the *meaning* — and, beyond that, something pertaining to the noetic, and not the psychic, dimension of man. — Viktor Frankl, *From Death Camp to Existentialism,* 102.

According to logotherapy, the striving to a meaning in one's own life is the primary motivational force in man. — Frankl, *Man's Search for Meaning.*

It is, of course, not the aim of logotherapy to take the place of existing psycho-therapy, but only to complement it . . . which includes the spiritual dimension. — Frankl, *Doctor of the Soul.*

Thus logotherapy is a personalistic psycho-therapy which does not concern itself primarily with symptoms, but rather tries to bring about a change in orientation with respect to the symptoms. The therapeutic aim of logotherapy is to make the individual aware of his purpose in life and to bring him to a fuller understanding of it.

Logotherapy is based on the observation that uncertainty about life's meaning is one of the most important causes of emotional problems in the world today. It is optimistic about the prospects for individual emotional recovery, affirming the proposition that "the so-called life not worth living does not exist."

One example, according to Frankl, of a mistaken life-goal is the so-called "pleasure principle." "Pleasure," he states, "is not the goal of our aspirations, but the consequence of attaining them. . . . Men do not want pleasure, they simply want what they want. . . . When we set up pleasure as the whole meaning of life, we insure that in the final analysis, life shall inevitably

123

seem meaningless. Pleasure cannot possibly lend meaning to
life. For what is pleasure? A condition."

Logotherapy, like other therapies, is basically a form of
education. What is distinctive about logotherapy is that it not
only takes into account the two familiar factors in human
development, *heredity* and *environment,* but also the factor of
decision. "In the end, education must be education toward the
ability to decide."

See Also: Psychology; Subjectivity.

LOVE: (from the Old English *lēof,* dear; Latin *lubere,* to please;
from the Sanskrit *lubhyati,* he desires)

1. According to Nietzsche,

Love *as passion* —which is our European specialty — simply
must be of noble origin: as is well known, its invention must
be credited to the Provencal knight-poets, those magnificent
and inventive human beings of the "gay science" to whom
Europe owes so many things and almost owes itself. — Friedrich Nietzsche, *Beyond Good and Evil,* 208.

It is possible that underneath the holy fable and disguise of
Jesus' life there lies concealed one of the most painful cases
of the martyrdom of *knowledge about love:* the martyrdom
of the most innocent and desirous heart, never sated by any
human love; *demanding* love, to be loved and nothing else,
with hardness, with insanity, with terrible eruptions against
those who denied him love; the story of a poor fellow,
unsated and insatiable in love, who had to invent hell in
order to send to it those who did not *want* to love him— and
who finally, having gained knowledge about human love, had
to invent a god who is all love, all *ability* to love —who has
mercy on human love because it is so utterly wretched and
unknowing. Anyone who feels that way, who *knows* this
about love — *seeks* death. — *Ibid.,* 220.

The chastest words I have heard: "In true love it is the soul that envelops the body." — *Ibid.,* 89.

2. Jaspers writes that one of the elements of philosophical faith is "love as the fundamental actualization of the eternal in man." To this end, a sympathy must be maintained even for those forms of knowledge, such as myths, which have been rejected by philosophy:

Mythological categories contain a truth that strikes us with irresistible evidence when the chaff is separated from the grain. To ignore this truth, is to impovrish one's soul, to create a vacuum. A man who has lost his ear for such language seems no longer capable of love. For if the transcendent has become entirely nonsensuous, it no longer holds for him an object of love. — Karl Jaspers, *The Perennial Scope of Philosophy,* 142, 143.

3. In Tillich's view,

Love is always love; that is its static and absolute side. But love is always dependent on that which is loved, and therefore it is unable to force finite elements on finite existence in the name of an assumed absolute. The absoluteness of love is its power to go into the concrete situation, to discover what is demanded by the predicament of the concrete to which it turns. Therefore, love can never become fanatical in a fight for an absolute, or cynical under the impact of the relative. — Paul Tillich, *Systematic Theology,* I, 152.

One of the reasons for this misunderstanding of love is the identification of love with emotion. Love, like every human experience, of course includes an emotional element, and this can in the case of love prove to be overwhelmingly strong. But this element is not the whole of love. Above all, love as *agape* is far removed from pity, although it can have elements of pity within a particular situation. Nietzsche's attack on the Christian idea of love is caused by this confusion. But it should serve to warn the Christian church to demonstrate in teaching, preaching, and liturgy the unconditional demand for justice in the very nature of *agape*. . . .

Agape is a quality of love, that quality which expresses the self-transcendence of the religious element in love. If love is the ultimate norm of all moral demands, its *agape* quality points to the transcendent source of the content of the moral imperative. For *agape* transcends the finite possibilities of man. . . .

Agape as the self-transcending element of love is not separated from the other elements that usually are described as *epithymia* — the *libido* quality of love, *philia* — the friendship quality of love, and *eros* — the mystical quality of love. In all of them what we have called "the urge toward the reunion of the separated" is effective, and all of them stand under the judgment of *agape*. For love is one, even if one of its qualities predominates. — Tillich, *Morality and Beyond*, 39, 40.

4. According to Sartre,

Love is a conflict. . . . Why does the lover want to be *loved?* If Love were in fact a pure desire for physical possession, it could in many cases be easily satisfied. Proust's hero, for example, who installs his mistress in his home, who can see her and possess her at any hour of the day, who has been able to make her completely dependent on him economically, ought to be free from worry. Yet we know that he is, on the contrary, continually gnawed by anxiety. Through her consciousness Albertine escapes Marcel even when he is at her side, and that is why he knows relief only when he gazes on her while she sleeps. It is certain then that the lover wishes to capture a "consciousness." — Jean-Paul Sartre, *Being and Nothingness*, 342.

The lover does not desire to possess the beloved as one possesses a thing; he demands a special type of appropriation. He wants to possess a freedom as freedom.

On the other hand, the lover can not be satisfied with that superior form of freedom which is a free and voluntary engagement. Who would be content with a love given as pure loyalty to a sworn oath? Who would be satisfied with the words, "I love you because I have freely engaged myself to love you and because I do not wish to go back on my word." Thus the lover demands a pledge, yet is irritated by a pledge. — *Ibid.,* 343.

5. Marcel writes:

We love only insofar as we do not try to know. Love is always a belief. The supreme truth of the myth of Psyche is precisely that thought, when seeking to determine the content of love, ceases to be free. All this we knew already; but what we discover, it seems, is that thought affirms, as it were, the possibility of an ineffable echo in God, of an act by which God re-creates it in love, and by a bold and creative transposition individuality somehow takes possession again of that which it had seemed to abandon as alien to its essential nature and posits itself as a creature (by the act which posits the non-contingency of its particular experience). A true spiritual life begins only with the affirmation of a reciprocity in God, of a response, and this affirmation is prayer. — Gabriel Marcel, *Philosophical Fragments,* 101, 102.

M

MAN: (from the Sanscrit *manu,* human being, man)

Existentialists from their view of man by beginning with the fact that the individual is always the existent-in-the-world, already *in encounter.* Generally speaking, they hold that there is no such thing as a *pure subject.*

1. Kierkegaard's view of man can be viewed as similar to that of the classical Greek philosophers. Man is a unit composed of three parts: (1) the soul, (2) the body, and (3) the spirit, or self. By "soul" he means the intellect, or reason. By "body" he means sense-perceptions or sensuousness, the Danish masking an ambiguity. By "spirit" or "self" he means self-consciousness or will.

When the personality is in equilibrium, the "spirit" or self unites soul and body, and the man lives in harmony (c.f. *The Concept of Dread,* the *Sickness Unto Death).*

When the personality is not in equilibrium, man lives out of balance and out of harmony. This happens when man sins, sin being caused by dread. Dread is of two kinds, objective and subjective. Objective dread is original sin, from the Fall of Adam. Subjective dread is the sin we acquire as we grow up. Dread serves a positive purpose, being the first step toward finding oneself again and regaining equilibrium.

As Kierkegaard's thought progressed into the third stage of his life and literary production, he developed in more detail his conception of the social nature of man:

Sociality is part of the definition of man as an animal. — Søren Kierkegaard, *The Last Years,* 170.
Man is an animal who can become spirit, a fate which as

an animal he is more afraid of than of dying. — *Ibid.*, 132.

Kierkegaard's conception of the Individual *(q.v.)* was not a dogmatic individualism but rather an instrumental individualism. Kierkegaard was not preaching the doctrine that only one single thing exists in the world, the individual soul. Kierkegaard was not a Solipsist. Rather, his doctrine of individualism was intended to serve a purpose, specifically to provide a corrective to the depersonalizing tendencies of the day.

2. Nietzsche:

In Genoa one evening, in the twilight, I heard from a tower a long chiming of bells; it was never like to end, and sounded as if insatiable above the noise of the streets, out into the evening sky and sea-air, so thrilling, and at the same time so childish and so sad. I then remembered the words of Plato, and suddenly felt the force of them in my heart: *"Human matters, one and all, are not worthy of great seriousness; nevertheless. . . ."* — Friedrich Nietzsche, *Human, All-Too-Human,* 395.

Until the advent of the ascetic ideal, man, the animal *man,* had no meaning at all on this earth. His existence was aimless. — Nietzsche, *The Genealogy of Morals,* 298.

Let me repeat, now that I have reached the end, what I said at the beginning: man would sooner have the void for his purpose than be void of purpose. — *Ibid.,* 299.

3. Berdyaev, striving for more philosophical balance, says

It is indisputable that man is a social being, but he is also spiritual being. He belongs to two worlds. It is only as a spiritual being that man can know the good as such. As a social being he knows only the changing conceptions about the good. A sociology which denies that man is a spiritual being, deriving his valuations from the spiritual world, is not a science but a false philosophy and even a false religion. — Nicolas Berdyaev, *The Destiny of Man,* 21.

The essential and fundamental problem is the problem of man — of his knowledge, his freedom, his creativeness. Man is the key to the mystery of knowledge and of existence. — *Ibid.*, 11.

4. Jaspers diverges from several other Existentialists, especially Sartre and Kierkegaard, in saying

This finiteness as existence means that even as himself man cannot ascribe himself to himself. It is not through himself that he is originally himself. — Karl Jaspers, *The Perennial Scope of Philosophy*, 64.

The idea is fallacious, Jaspers writes, that

To know what man is, is the only knowledge that is possible for us, for we are men ourselves — and that alone is essential — for man is the measure of all things. — *Ibid.*, 47.

The reason is:

Though what is must become actual for man, since for him all being lies in presence, it is not brought forth by man; man produces neither sensible realities, nor the content of his ideas, his thoughts and symbols. — *Ibid.*, 48.

So far as the origin of man is concerned,

Man cannot be derived from something else, but is immediately at the base of all things. To be aware of this signifies man's freedom, which is lost in every other total determination of his being. — *Ibid.*, 59.

For example,

The matter was admirably summed up by a joke that appeared in *Simplicissimus* during the first World War. Two Bavarian peasants are talking things over. People are pretty dumb, says one, maybe Darwin was right after all. Maybe we are descended from the apes. — Yes, says the other, but just the same I'd like to see the ape that first noticed that he wasn't an ape any more. — *Ibid.*, 59.

131

5. Tillich makes the question of man the basis for the organization of his entire *Systematic Theology*, the summation of his own life's work.

> In so far as man's existence has the character of self-contradiction or estrangement, a double consideration is demanded, one side dealing with man as he essentially is (and ought to be) and the other dealing with what he is in his self-estranged existence (and should not be). These correspond to the Christian distinction between the realm of salvation. — Paul Tillich, *Systematic Theology*, I, 66.

6. Heidegger, like Nietzsche and Jaspers, describes immediate experience in terms of both finitude and guilt. Existence is tragic. *Verfallenheit*, being lost and a prey to existence, is guilt.

> Being guilty is not the result of a guilty act, but conversely, the act is possible only because of an original "being guilty."
> — Martin Heidegger, *Being and Time*, 284.

7. According to Sartre,

> Man is a useless passion. — Jean-Paul Sartre, *Being and Nothingness*.

> Man is condemned to be free. — *Ibid*.

> Hell is — other people! — Sartre, *No Exit*, 47.

See Also: Existence; Freedom; Human Nature; Subjectivity.

MARCEL, GABRIEL (1889-   ): Born in Paris on the 7th of December, 1889, Gabriel Marcel's father became the French representative to Sweden in 1898. His Jewish mother died when Gabriel was four.

He graduated from the Sorbonne in 1910 with a doctorate. The process philosophy of Bergson, popular at the time, was balanced in Marcel's mind by F. H. Bradley's idealistic book, *Appearance and Reality*.

Becoming seriously ill in 1912, he went to Switzerland to recover, beginning his *Journal métaphysique*, published in 1927. He served with the Red Cross during the First World War. His first play, *Le Soleil invisible*, was written during this period.

Marcel's thought became a sort of metaphysical journey toward the acceptance of Christianity. In the course of his work as the drama critic for *L'Europe nouvelle*, he reviewed one of François Mauriac's works sympathetically. Mauriac replied by asking, "Why are you not one of us? (a Catholic)" Soon afterward, Marcel formally joined the church.

His major works include some twenty plays, including *Rome n'est plus dans Rome*, 1951, about a professor and his wife who leave France for Brazil out of fear that communism is about to overrun the country. Other important works are *Être et avoir*, 1935 *(Being and Having*, 1949), *Présence et immortalité*, 1959, *Le Mystère de l'être (The Mystery of Being*, 1950-51), *Homo Viator*, 1945 (English 1951), *Les Hommes contre l'humain*, 1951 *(Man Against Mass Society*, 1952), *Le Déclin de la sagesse*, 1954 *(The Decline of Wisdom*, 1954), and *Fragments philosophiques 1909-1914 (Philosophical Fragments*, 1962).

Marcel is critical of Sartre for saying that man chooses his own values. Rather, in the construction of personality, fears and desires belong only to the realm of having, whereas the realm of being is reached when both individuals cooperate with the freedom of the other in love, without using the other either as a means for emotional satisfaction or self-discovery and increased self-love. Ultimately, only God can be said to be pure and perfect being, whereas creatures always are seen to have a greater or lesser degree of having.

N

NAUSEA: (from the Greek *nausia, nautia,* seasickness).

The title of Sartre's famous novel of solipsistic despair, and the name Sartre uses for man's reaction in experiencing the absurd world. Both the physical world and the realization of their own uselessness give men the feeling of revulsion which Sartre calls nausea.

> 1. The word absurdity is coming to life under my pen; a little while ago, in the garden, I couldn't find it, but neither was I looking for it, I didn't need it: I thought without words, *on* things, *with* things. Absurdity was not an idea in my head, or the sound of a voice, only this long serpent dead at my feet, this wooden serpent. Serpent or claw or root or vulture's talon, what difference does it make. And without formulating anything clearly, I understood that I had found the key to Existence, the key to my Nauseas, to my own life. In fact, all that I could grasp beyond that returns to this fundamental absurdity. — Jean-Paul Sartre, *Nausea,* 173.

2. The "serpent" mentioned above, or the "wrinkled paw" below was the root of a tree which he was contemplating. He was struck most of all by its absurdity, which caused him to feel revulsion, nausea.

> But faced with this great wrinkled paw, neither ignorance nor knowledge was important: the world of explanations and reasons is not the world of existence. A circle is not absurd, it is clearly explained by the rotation of a straight segment around one of its extremities. But neither does a

circle exist. This root, on the other hand, existed in such a way that I could not explain it. Knotty, inert, nameless, it fascinated me, filled my eyes, brought me back unceasingly to its own existence. In vain to repeat: "This is a root" — it didn't work any more. I saw clearly that you could not pass from its function as a root, as a breathing pump, *to that,* to this hard and compact skin of a sea lion, to this oily, callous, headstrong look. The function explained nothing: it allowed you to understand generally that it was a root, but not *that one* at all. This root, with its colour, shape, its congealed movement, was . . . below all explanation. Each of its qualities escaped it a little, flowed out of it, half solidified, almost became a thing; each one was *in the way* in the root and the whole stump now gave me the impression of unwinding itself a little, denying its existence to lose itself in a frenzied excess. — *Ibid.,* 174, 175.

3. Then the Nausea seized me, I dropped to a seat, I no longer knew where I was; I saw the colours spin slowly around me, I wanted to vomit. And since that time, the Nausea has not left me, it holds me. — *Ibid.,* 30.

4. The Nausea has not left me and I don't believe it will leave me so soon; but I no longer have to bear it, it is no longer an illness or a passing fit: it is I. — *Ibid.,* 170.

See Also: Sartre.

NIETZSCHE, FRIEDRICH (1844-1900): One of the most brilliant and original of the Existentialist thinkers, Nietzsche continues to be one of the major influences on modern thought. Born on the 15th of October, 1844, in Röcken, Prussian Saxony, his father was a Lutheran pastor. When he was five years old his father died, in 1849. The family had to move, and young Friedrich was brought up in the feminine and pious society of his mother, sister, grandmother, and two aunts.

From 1854 to 1858 he studied at the local Gymnasium, and from 1858 to 1864 was a pupil at the celebrated Pforta boarding-school. He was a passionate admirer of Greek genius, especially Plato and Aeschylus. He tried his hand at poetry and music, being greatly influenced by Hölderlin.

In October of the year 1864 he entered the University of Bonn, transferring the next autumn to Leipzig, where studied philology under the famous Ritschl. He was attracted by the atheism of the writings of Schopenhauer.

Having become Ritschl's favorite pupil, Nietzsche was recommended for appointment to the University of Basel even before he had received the doctorate. In May of 1869, at twenty-four, he delivered his inaugural lecture, "Homer and Classical Philology." Upon the outbreak of the Franco-Prussian War, he joined the ambulance corps of the Prussian army. He was injured in the chest during the war, and was medically discharged.

Returning to Basel, he spent a great deal of time visiting his friend, Richard Wagner, at his villa on Lake Lucerne. Wagner was the age Nietzsche's father would have been, and Wagner appreciated him so long as he did not disagree with him. He was enthusiastic about his first book, *Die Geburt der Tragödie aus dem Geiste der Musik,* 1872 *(The Birth of Tragedy From the Spirit of Music),* a book which contrasted Greek culture before and after Socrates, to the detriment of Socrates. Contemporary German culture strongly resembled Greek culture after Socrates, and could only be saved if permeated by the spirit of Wagner, he argued. Classical philologists were not as enthusiastic as Wagner about the book.

Unzeitgemässe Betrachtungen (Untimely Meditations, or *Thoughts Out of Season),* four essays, appeared between 1873 and 1876.

After 1876, Nietzsche and Wagner broke, Nietzsche thinking just as poorly of *Parsifal* as Wagner thought of the new *Human, All-Too-Human (Menschliches, Allzumenschliches,* 1878). Positivistic in character, the new book attacks metaphysics by showing how the metaphysical superstructures can be explained materialistically. For example, the moral distinction between good and evil had its origin in the utilitarian consideration that some actions were beneficial to society while others harmed it, although with time this origin of morality was forgotten. Again, conscience originates merely as the belief in authority: it is not the voice of God but of parents and teachers.

The break with Wagner marks the beginning of the second period in Nietzsche's thought. In this second phase he values Socrates more highly, whereas before he had criticized and denounced Socrates as a rationalist. In the second, he prefers science above poetry, while in the first he had written that culture finds its justification only in the production of a genius, the creative artist, poet, and musician. Nietzsche questions every accepted belief, as had the philosophers of the French Enlightenment.

In the Spring of 1879, a combination of ill health and disgust led Nietzsche to resign from his position at Basel. Thus began "the ten years," which were to see the production of his major works. He led a wandering life, seeking health in the resorts of Switzerland, Italy, and Germany, especially at the Engadine and the Riviera. His books were written in complete isolation, and despite such ills as severe headaches and partial blindness. Once written, the works were completely ignored by the public.

1881 saw the production of *Morgenröte (The Dawn)*, opening his campaign against the morality of self-denial. When he sent a copy to a former friend, Rohde, he did not acknowledge its receipt.

Die Fröliche Wissenschaft, 1882 *(The Gay Science*, or *Joyful Wisdom)* argues that Christianity in all its aspects is hostile to life. Beginning with the report that God is dead, new and vast horizons are opened to free spirits. The idea of the "eternal recurrence" came to Nietzsche with the force of an inspiration. In infinite time there must be periodic cycles in which all that has once been is repeated again.

Nietzsche proposed marriage to several women, one of whom, Lou Salomé, meant a great deal to him in 1882. His sister, Elisabeth, intrigued to break up the romance, however, and soon he was more alone than ever.

Thus Spake Zarathustra (Also Sprach Zarathustra) was written at this time, the first two sections appearing in 1883, the third

137

In 1884, and the fourth, which was intended to be an interlude before the other sections of the book, in 1885. The lack of response to this first attempt of his to present the whole of his thought discouraged Nietzsche, and he abandoned the work at this point. The book contains his mayor doctrines: eternal recurrence, the super-man, and the transvaluation of values.

Afterwards, he wrote *Jenseits von Gut und Böse*, 1886 *(Beyond Good and Evil)*, and *Zur Genealogie der Moral*, 1887 *(The Genealogy of Morals)*. After the publication of this last book Nietzsche was sent a letter of appreciation by the Danish critic, Georg Brandes, who lectured the next year on Nietzsche's writings at the University of Copenhagen. This began to develop public interest in his ideas, so that within ten years Nietzsche was famous.

1888 was the year in which his self-interpretation, *Ecce Homo*, was written, though his sister withheld it until 1908. This was followed by *Der Fall Wagner (The Wagner Case)*, a ferocious attack on his former friend. *Der Antichrist (The Antichrist)* was the first part of what he intended to be his major work, to be entitled *Umwertung aller Werte (Revaluation of All Values)*. *Götzen-Dämmerung, oder Wie man mit dem Hammer philosophirt (Twilight of the Idols)* was written earlier that year, while his last effort was to assemble some of his choicest passages under the title, *Nietzsche contra Wagner*.

Der Wille Zur Macht (The Will to Power), published by his sister in 1895-1905, 1901, and 1906, presents a special problem. Although he had for a while meant to make this the title of his magnum opus, the book as published consists of a collection of his earlier notes, some of them revised in later of his works.

During the year 1888, Nietzsche began to show definite signs of madness. In January of 1889 he suffered a complete breakdown. He was taken from Turin to a clinic at Basel, but never really recovered. After some treatment he went to his mother's home in Naumburg. After his mother died, he lived at Weimar with his sister. By this time he was famous, but he was in no position to appreciate that fact. His illness, never conclusively diagnosed, was probably an atypical general paralysis. It seems probable that, despite the attempts of his sister to deny it, he had contracted a syphilitic infection as a university student, or possibly during the war while caring for sick soldiers, and that the disease finally affected the brain. He died on the 25th of August, 1900.

P

PARADOXICAL INTENTION: Frankl's term for one of the procedural methods in treatment of mental illness on existential-psychoanalytic principles. It refers to the paradoxical wish which the patient may use to take the place of his fears.

As soon as the patient stops fighting his obsessions and instead tries to ridicule them by dealing with them in an ironical way, by applying paradoxical intention, the vicious circle is out. — Victor Frankl, *Man's Search for Meaning.*

PHENOMENOLOGY: The precursor to contemporary Existentialism, greatly influencing Heidegger and Sartre. Husserl was the key phenomenologist, and attempted to construct a philosophy of pure subjectivism to oppose naturalism. Phenomenology is a descriptive philosophy which "brackets" existence, paying careful attention to the structure of experience as it appears, rather than attempting initially to account for that appearance in terms of essence.

The gap between pure consciousness and the world of ordinary experience is bridged by means of the concept of a "pre-given life-world."

PHILOSOPHICAL ANTHROPOLOGY: Sartre's term for the new science which he believes is needed to properly understand man. The existing tools and methods of the sciences — natural science, traditional sociology, anthropology — are not adequate for the task.

141

The basis for this philosophical anthropology is a new kind of reason, the conception of which he proposes to develop in the *Critique of Dialectical Reason.*

See also: Sartre; Praxis.

PRAXIS: Sartre uses this Greek word, which means "deed" or "action," to refer to any purposeful human activity. The whole structure of the *Critique of Dialectical Reason* depends on the notion of "praxis," that is, man's action in the world, his work, and his rational intention in the material universe.

The *Critique of Dialectical Reason* starts from experience, from the experience of each individual that he is capable of freely intervening in the world in "praxis," and that "praxis" is able — by means of the dialectical struggle — to replace the present by a *forseen* future.

This is necessarily dialectical in form. It proceeds by the clash and the overcoming of contradictions. By this sort of analysis, it will be seen that each individual act is a part of the dialectical process. We are aware of this part of our experience, of this character of our experience, by our understanding of "praxis."

These ideas can be both contrasted and compared with Sartre's earlier thought, represented by *Being and Nothingness,* for example. *Being and Nothingness* represents a more individualistic and personal standpoint than the *Critique of Dialectical Reason,* with its Marxist sociology. The first is the more primitive level of individual self-interest, while the second is the more advanced level of interest in oneself as a member of a group or community.

See also: Sartre; Philosophical Anthropology.

PSYCHOLOGY: Existential interest in the theory of man has led to its formulation of a psychological theory which is distinctive. Sartre, Jaspers, and others of the philosophical Existentialists have written a great deal on the topic.

In Europe, there are four explicitly Existential psycho-therapists, who are (1) Victor Frankl, the Viennese neuropsychiatrist, founder of "Logotherapy," (2) Ludwig Binswanger, the Swiss psychiatrist, founder of "Existential Analysis," (3) Medard Boss, also a Swiss psychiatrist ,who calls his therapy "Daseinanalysis," and (4) Hans Trüb, Swiss, who calls his therapy "anthropological."

1. Jaspers, who came to his interest in philosophy from a medical background, has written:

> It now occurred to me that a cause of the intellectual confusion lay in the very nature of the subject itself. For the object of psychiatry was man, not merely his body, perhaps his body least of all, but rather his mind, his personality, he himself. I read not merely the somatic dogma: mental diseases are diseases of the brain (Griesinger), but also the tenet: mental diseases are diseases of personality (Schüle).
> — Karl Jaspers, *The Philosophy of Karl Jaspers,* 17.

2. Sartre has exhibited a deep interest in psychological topics, both from a descriptive and a prescriptive point of view:

> Thus existential psychoanalysis is *moral description,* for it releases to us the ethical meaning of various human projects.
> — Jean-Paul Sartre, *Being and Nothingness,* 544.

> Existential psychoanalysis is going to reveal to man the real goal of his pursuit, which is being as a synthetic fusion of the in-itself with the for-itself; existential psychoanalysis is going to acquaint man with his passion. — *Ibid.*

> It amounts to the same thing whether one gets drunk alone or is a leader of nations. If one these activities takes precedence over the other, this will not be because of its real goal but because of the degree of consciousness which it possesses of its ideal goal; and in this case it will be the quietism of the solitary drunkard which will take precedence over the vain agitation of the leader of nations. — *Ibid.,* 545.

> Ontology and existential psychoanalysis (or the spontaneous and empirical application which men have always made of

these disciplines) must reveal to the moral agent that he is *the being by whom values exist.* It is then that his freedom will become conscious of itself and will reveal itself in anguish as the unique source of value and the nothingness by which the *world* exists. — Ibid., 545.

3. Tillich, rather than forging principles for a new approach to the human personality, is more concerned to analyze the basis and character of previous therapies:

Recently the term "insight" has been given connotations of *gnosis,* namely, of a knowledge which transforms and heals. Depth psychology attributes healing powers to insight, meaning not a detached knowledge of psychoanalytic theory or of one's own past in the light of this theory but a repetition of one's actual experiences with all the pains and horrors of such a return. Insight in this sense is a reunion with one's own past and especially with those moments in it which influence the present destructively. Such a cognitive union produces a transformation just as radical and as difficult as that presupposed and demanded by Socrates and Paul. For most of the Asiatic philosophies and religion the uniting, healing, and transforming power of knowledge is a matter of course. — Paul Tillich, *Systematic Theology,* I, 96.

4. Frankl, the leading exponent of Existential psychology, defines his own conception of therapy:

Logotherapy focusses on man's search for the meaning of human existence. Such a search is an important undertaking in psychotherapy since, as can easily be understood, existential frustration can lead to neurotic disease. It can become pathogenous in the sense of creating neuroses. But man's concern about a meaning in life which would be worthy of life is in itself not a sign of disease. — Victor Frankl, *From Death Camp to Existentialism,* 100, 101.

The dream of half a century has centered around mechanisms to explain, and techniques to treat, neurotic diseases. I deem that this dream has been dreamt out. What is needed now is that doctors abandon seeing man as a machine and learn, instead, to see behind the disease the human being: Homo patiens. For if psychotherapy and education aim to cope with existential frustration — this world-wide collective neurosis — they must free themselves from any nihilistic philosophy of man and focus their attention upon man's longing and groping for a higher meaning in life. — *Ibid.,* 111.

What logotherapy calls man's "will-to-meaning" is a reality, and a primary reality. Only in exceptional cases does it represent something like a "secondary rationalization." — *Ibid.,* 98.

Contrary to Sartre, Frankl says

I think the meaning of our existence is not invented by ourselves but rather detected. — Frankl, *Man's Search for Meaning.*

It is life itself that asks question of man. . . . It is not up to man to question; rather he should recognize that he is questioned, questioned by life. — Frankl, *The Doctor and the Soul.*

Ultimately, man should not ask himself, "What is the meaning of my life?" but should, instead, realize that it is not up to him to question — it is he who *is* questioned, questioned by life; it is he who has to answer, by answering for life. His role is to respond — to be responsible. — Frankl, *From Death Camp to Existentialism,* 107.

The proper attitude of the therapist toward the patient is described in these ways:

Since the logotherapist interprets his job mainly as the very education to responsibility, to the full awareness and consciousness of the very essence of human existence (i.e., responsibleness), he will certainly not impose his own values on the patient. — *Ibid.,* 103.

The categoric imperative of logotherapy can be put thus: Live as if you were living for the second time and as if you had acted as wrongly the first time as you are about to act now. — *Ibid.,* 107.

5. Binswanger notes that
What we psychiatrists judge and label from the outside as a striking, bizarre, morbid "act of a schizophrenic" can be understood existential-analytically as often the last attempt of the existence to come to itself! — Ludwig Binswanger, *The Case of Ellen West*, 311.

R

REASON: (from the Latin *ratio,* reason, computation; akin to Greek *arariskein,* to fit, joining, the source word for "arm")

1. Kierkegaard uses reason in two senses: (1) discursively, as the normal, everyday type of reasoning, reasoning for the sake of a definite conclusion, and (2) as it is in a faith-philosophy, as a term for all the creative processes of the mind, including imagination and esthetic judgment.

Kierkegaard considers Socrates to be the best example of a truly subjective thinker. One can only know oneself by inwardness, which is an attitude of infinite passion toward self-revelation. Inwardness is seen as opposed to Mediation, or the general Hegelian method of approach to reality through the rational. Inwardness is attained through despair *(q.v.).*

In his indirect works (the esthetic works, the first division of his "authorship") Kierkegaard attacks what he terms "abstract thought," that is, thought which treats the existing thinker as an "accident" which can safely be overlooked in the approach to general truth. What Hegel believed to be a "totality" of thought Kierkegaard said was a "mere abstraction."

2. Nietzsche writes:

"From where do I get the concept of thinking? Why do I believe in cause and effect? What gives me the right to speak of an ego, and even of an ego as cause, and finally of an ego as the cause of thought?" — Friedrich Nietzsche, *Beyond Good and Evil,* 24.

In certain cases, as the proverb points out, one only *remains* a philosopher by being — silent. — Nietzsche, *Human, All-Too-Human*, 12.

Everything has evolved; there are *no eternal facts,* as there are likewise no absolute truths. Therefore, *historical philosophising* is henceforth necessary, and with it the virtue of diffidence. — *Ibid.*, 15.

The illogical is necessary for man, and that out of the illogical comes much that is good. . . . Even the most rational man has need of nature again from time to time, *i.e.* his *illogical fundamental attitude* towards all things. — *Ibid.*, 46.

3. According to Jaspers,

Philosophy cannot give us truth, but it can illuminate, direct attention, remove the cataract from our mind's eye, as it were. Actual vision and realization is up to every individual. — Karl Jaspers, *Existentialism and Humanism*, 96.

Reason relates all the various meanings of truth to one another, by asserting each one. It prevents any truth from being confined to itself. . . . Reason forbids fixation in any truth-meaning that does not embrace all truth. — Jaspers, *The Perennial Scope of Philosophy*, 43.

Reason is the Comprehensive in us; it does not flow from the primal source of being, but is an instrument of existence. It is the existential absolute that serves to actualize the primal source and bring it to the widest manifestation. — *Ibid.*, 44.

Reason is the bond that unites all the modes of the Comprehensive. It allows no existent to separate itself absolutely, to sink into isolation, to be reduced to nothingness by fragmentation. — *Ibid.*, 45.

Reason demands boundless *communication,* it is itself the total will to communicate. — *Ibid.*

4. In Tillich's view,

We can distinguish between an ontological and a technical concept of reason. The former is predominant in the classical tradition from Parmenides to Hegel; the latter, though always present in pre-philosophical and philosophical thought, has become predominant since the breakdown of German classical idealism and in the wake of English empiricism. According to the classical philosophical tradition, reason is the structure of the mind which enables the mind to grasp and to transform reality. . . . (According to) the technical concept of reason, reason is reduced to the capacity for "reasoning". — Paul Tillich, *Systematic Theology*, I, 72, 73.

Ontological reason can be defined as the structure of the mind which enables it to grasp and to shape reality. — *Ibid.*, 75.

Subjective reason is the structure of the mind which enables it to grasp and to shape reality on the basis of a corresponding structure of reality (in whatever way this correspondence may be explained). — *Ibid.*, 76.

S

SARTRE, JEAN-PAUL (1905-   ): The leading French Existentialist, philosopher, playwright, and novelist, Jean-Paul Sartre was born in Paris on the 21st of June, 1905. Orphaned early in life, he was raised by his grandfather, Charles Schweitzer (an uncle of Albert Schweitzer), who considered him to be a child prodigy.

He was educated at the École Normale Supérieure. In 1929, by the age of twenty-four, he had earned a Ph. D. in philosophy.

Before the Second World War he taught at various schools in the provinces, including the Lycée at Le Havre, the Lycée Henri IV, and the Lycée Condorcet in 1935, resigning in 1942.

In 1933-4 he studied at the Institut Français is Berlin. The philosophies of Husserl and Heidegger were his main interest, while there. He has been criticized for spending time in Berlin under Hitler, calmly reading Husserl without realizing that the philosopher with whose works he was occupied was no longer permitted access to the library of his university, being prohibited from doing so by his most prominent pupil, Heidegger, a partisan of the Third Reich. (— François Bondy, *Neue Zürcher Zeitung,* 182nd vol., January 5, 1961, Nº 412).

His major works began with such significant articles as "L'Ange du morbide," (1923) in *Revue sans titre,* "Légende de la vérité," (1931) in *Bifur. L'Imagination* was published in 1936 *(Imagination,* University of Michigan, 1962), followed by "La transcendance de l'Ego" in 1937 *(Transcendence of the Ego,* Noonday, 1957).

151

With the publication of *La Nausée* in 1938 *(Nausea,* New Directions, 1949), the first stage in Sarte's thought can be said to begin. This may be called the stage of *solipsistic despair.* Marooned within himself, unable to prove the existence of other persons, one has contact with the world only through the emotion of Nausea, occasioned by the absurdity of existence. This mood is also found in such short stories as *Le Mur,* 1939 *(The Wall), La Chambre (The Room), Érostrate, Intimité,* and *L'Enfance d'un chef (The Wall and Other Stories,* New Directions, 1948).

Esquisse d'une théorie des émotions, 1939, *(The Emotions, Outline of a Theory,* Philosophical Library, 1948) is an analysis of the roles of fear, lust, melancholy and anguish in man's life, looking toward the true reality of conscious life. The book is an excellent application of the phenomenological method which Sartre had learned in Berlin.

L'Imaginaire, psychologie phénoménologique de l'imagination, 1940, *(Psychology of Imagination,* Philosophical Library, 1948) states that our consciousness is able to produce mental images spontaneously. In other words, consciousness asserts itself not only in perceiving the real but also in calling forth the imaginary.

II

The second stage of Sartre's thought is the *negative spirit of resistance,* typified by his major philosophical book, *L'Être et le néant,* 1943 *(Being and Nothingness,* Philosophical Library, 1956).

During the years from 1939 to 1941 he had served in the army, was captured and spent nine months as a prisoner of war in Germany. When released, he returned to Paris and joined the resistance movement, together with Albert Camus and François Mauriac. In 1944, he was caught and imprisoned by the Nazis. These experiences led Sartre to think that freedom is total responsibility in total solitude, because a member of the resistance who was caught could not claim his "rights" or expect outside help. He had to learn for himself how much torture he could stand. In such a world of intrigue and deception the only support was internal. Thus the limits of man's freedom, under such conditions, became his personal capacity for resisting torture and death.

Being and Nothingness is a tremendous attempt to construct a theory of Being on Existential terms, with a distinctively individualistic tone. The first attitude toward others is love, language, and masochism. The second attitude toward others, he declares, is indifference, desire, hate, and sadism. The three classifications of Being are Being-in-itself, Being-for-itself, and Being-for-others *(qq.v.)*.

The dramatic works Sartre wrote during this period include *Les Mouches,* 1943, *(The Flies* in *No Exit and The Flies,* Knopf, 1947), *Huis-clos,* 1944 *(No Exit),* and *Morts sans sépulture,* 1946 *(The Victors* in *Three Plays,* Knopf, 1949).

III

The third stage in Sartre's thought is the optimistic humanism of *L'Existentialisme est un humanisme,* 1946 *(Existentialism,* Philosophical Library, 1947). A remarkable work, self-assured and brilliantly written, this lecture has been widely quoted for its famous definition of Existentialism: *"Existence* comes before *essence* — or, if you will, that we must begin from the subjective." It has also been widely criticized — for the same definition. Sartre is interested in examining the implications of the assertions that there is no God, that there is no fixed human nature, and that there are no a priori moral values.

Sartre's other novel was written during this period, *Les Chemins de la liberté,* 1945-49 *(Roads to Freedom),* a trilogy: (1) *L'Age de raison (The Age of Reason,* Knopf, 1947), set in Paris in 1938, with Mathieu as an ineffectual sort of anti-hero, a philosophy professor who writes one story a year; when his mistress becomes pregnant, he borrows and steals five thousand francs for an abortion, only to see her marry another so she can keep the child; (2) *Les Sursis (The Reprieve,* 1947), set during the week of the Munich crisis, the rape of Czechoslovakia, the French mobilization in that September of 1938, conveying the inner story of that week by different peoples' reaction; (3) *La Mort dans l'âme (Troubled Sleep,* 1951), in which Mathieu is transformed from ineffectuality by the stress of battle, becoming a military hero. A fourth volume was intended but only partially completed as *Drôle d'amitié (Strange Friendship,* 1949), describing how a non-conforming community is betrayed by party hacks during the days of the Soviet-Nazi pact.

The dramatic works written during these years include *Les Jeux sont faits,* 1947 *(The Chips Are Down,* Lear, 1948), *Les Mains sales,* 1948 *(Dirty Hands,* in *Three Plays,* Knopf, 1949), in which a young intellectual is torn between theories and actions, and whose general theme is that one who wants to do some good in the world must be willing to get his hands dirty; *L'Engrenage,* 1949 *(In the Mesh,* Dakers, 1954), *Le Diable et le Bon Dieu,* 1951 *(The Devil and the Good Lord and Two Other Plays,* Knopf, 1960), *Kean,* 1954 (d'après Alexandre Dumas), *Nekrassov,* 1955, *La Putain respectueuse (The Respectful Prostitute),* describing a Southern woman who tries without success to stop a lynching, then marries a wealthy man who promises her a house; *Les Séquestrés d'Altona,* 1960 *(The Condemned of Altona).*

During this exceptionally productive period of his life, various essays were published, such as *Situations I,* 1947, *II,* 1948, *III,* 1949 *(Literary and Philosophical Essays,* Philosophical Library, 1957), *La Liberté Cartésienne,* 1946, *Baudelaire,* 1947 *(Baudelaire,* Horizon, 1949), *Réflexions sur la question juive,* 1947 *(Anti-Semite and Jew,* Schocken, 1948), which contains some advice to Jews on political tactics, that they should stop trying to accommodate themselves to the movements of the Christian crowd and instead stand on his distinctive Jewishness, striking out at the two root causes of anti-semitism, class society and the bourgeois doctrine of private property; *Qu'est-ce que la littérature?,* 1948 *(What Is Literature?,* Philosophical Library, 1947), *Visages,* 1948, *Entretiens sur la politique,* 1949, *Saint Genet, comédien et martyr,* 1952 *(Saint Genet, Actor and Martyr,* Braziller, 1963), which is a psychological study of a remarkable poet Jean Genet, a homosexual with a police record; "Questions de méthode," in *Les Temps Modernes, XIII,* 1957 *(Search for a Method,* Knopf, 1963).

During these years after the Second World War, Sartre was editor of the monthly review, *Les Temps Modernes,* commenting on political and social issues. A political party that he helped found, the "Republican Democratic Rally," collapsed in 1952. During the Algerian War, he took an uncompromising stand against the attempt of France to keep any of her old colonies. Only his prestige kept him out of prison. He was called a traitor and his apartment was bombed.

IV

The fourth stage in Sartre's philosophical development is the publication of his sociological doctrine in the *Critique de la raison dialectique, I,* 1960. In his critique of dialectical reason, he attempts to combine the concepts of Existentialism with those of Marxism, and states that Existentialism can be a humanizing influence within the Marxist system of thought, dropping from Marxism such dated concepts as determinism.

Sartre has also provided an autobiography, *Les Mots,* 1964 (*The Words,* Braziller, 1964), for which he won the Nobel Prize for Literature for that year. He refused to accept the prize on the grounds that it was "a literary bribe."

Having rejected what he termed "bourgeois marriage," he formed while a student a love relationship with Simone de Beauvoir which has remained a settled partnership through life.

SOCIETY: (from the Latin *socius,* companion)

One famous passage attacking the social philosophy of existentialism, written by Bobbio, contains the following:

> Existentialism shuns society as being an obscure, inert mass, but it does not seek society as being an active union of thoughts and deeds. . . . Man as conceived by the existentialists has severed every link with a transcendent God, but he has not re-established contact with other men, his peers. He has remained isolated, shut up in his own finiteness — his own prisoner. — N. Bobbio, *The Philosophy of Decadentism,* 50.

He rejects the existential theory of society because

Society is debased to the status of the crowd or is raised to

155

that of a fellowship of "precious souls," but it is never actually encountered as an integral part of our individual lives. — Bobbio, *The Philosophy of Decadentism*, 50, 51.

He concludes his attack by writing that

> Existentialism is the philosophy of a worn-out generation; it flourishes in an age of great and ill-comprehended upheavals. . . . And when this world has fallen in ruins — and perhaps it already has fallen in ruins, or is about to do so — torn by its own contradictions, shattered by its lack of a system to which it may submit, then only will the existential philosopher be able to celebrate his triumph amid the ruins, like the ghost in a romantic ballad. And what else is the man whom existentialism portrays but a ghost that moves about amid the shadows — because he is a shadow himself — and does not fear death, but rather faces it unflinchingly, because he is himself already dead? For a world of dead men, a philosophy of ghosts. — Bobbio, *The Philosophy of Decadentism*, 52.

Existential thinkers do reject society, as is evident from such statements as Heidegger's "Society is the native land of fallen man," as Jaspers' more careful sentence that individual man "as existence must be continually 'in tension' with the objective institutions of society," and as Sartre's famous slogan that "Hell is — other people!" — Sartre's Hell-on-the-earth-in-society theme.

The reason for the existential rejection of society lies in the failure of essentialist philosophy to provide for a clearly non-repressive social organization, one which allows the individual freedom to develop. Essentialist philosophy has exaggerated the concept of morality, thinking it to be a kind of license for interference, a green light for the authorities to regulate the common people, a hunting stamp allowing the 'righteous' to oppress the 'wicked.'

Thus Berdyaev notes in a most perceptive passage:

> Rulers of states, hierarchs of churches, owners of business concerns, heads of families are not infrequently cruel not from

bloodthirstiness or a love of tyrannizing, but from atavistic moral emotions and a sense of duty which is a torture to themselves. — Berdyaev, *The Destiny of Man,* 90.

Society thus becomes the chief oppressor of the individual. To become an individual one must leave society, in one way or another. This was the conclusion of Kierkegaard after he noted the quality of cruelty which the society fastened upon the members of the family, church, and state.

Man is by nature one of the animal creation. Therefore all human effort tends towards herding together: 'let us unite,' etc. Naturally this happens under all sorts of high-sounding names, love and sympathy and enthusiasm, and the carrying out of some grand plan, and the like; this is the usual hypocrisy of the scoundrels we are. The truth is that in a herd we are free from the standard of the individual and ideal. — Kierkegaard, *The Last Years,* 31.

Freedom for the individual is possible only by becoming free from the restrictions of society, which is the animal organization of man at any rate—"the herd," or "the crowd." This is a theme which Nietzsche also developed, in speaking of the "transvaluation of values," by which the true individual would be freed from the restrictions of society.

Kierkegaard's description of actual society is based on the belief that secular social entities are the ethical expression of natural datum. Thus the family, the press, and the state are the expressions of the definition of man as animal. Marriage is the ethical expression of the propagation of the species. The daily press is viewed as "an immense abstraction" which wields the power of the crowd over the single individual. The state, which exists for the purpose of restraining crime rather than for the promotion of virtue, has as its highest aim the attainment of a kind of epicurean peace, a peace appropriate to the animal character of man rather than to his spiritual nature.

Kierkegaard's description of ideal society is based on the belief that the religious social entity — the church — by contrast expressed the spiritual basis of existence. In actual practice, however, the church ignored its spiritual constitution, suffering, in favor of temporal peace. This is the reason for Kierkegaard's denunciation of the actual church. However, Kierkegaard does not conclude that ideal society is utopian. That is, the church in an ideal or spiritual sense remains both possible and desirable.

The ambiguity in Kierkegaard's use of ideal is noted. On the one hand, actual society is in principle not ideal. Actual society can be ideal only in the sense of being the best of its type. But its type is in principle below the ideal in the spiritual sense. The actual is not a stage on the way to the ideal, but an expression of different, opposite principles. The actual not only fails, but fails necessarily. It is natural and numerical, not spiritual and individual.

Kierkegaard's contrast between the numerical and the unique or individual is basic to his social thought. By the numerical — or by "number" — Kierkegaard designates the numerable, the quantitative, whatever is not unique. In the numerical the differences between the members of a class can be ignored as accidental and unessential. Whenever the individual human being is treated as if he can be numbered, dehumanization is the result, as for example, in the "crowd."

It is notable that existentialism does not appear to have a clear social philosophy. This appears to be the result of its extreme individualism. Thus, Dostoevski was both a socialist and, later, a reactionary supporter of the crown. Heidegger betrayed Nazi sympathies. Sartre has embraced Marxism. However, it is misleading to conclude that existentialism has no basis for a theory of society on its own premises.

Existentialism criticizes any mediating social entities. Thus the individual is advised to keep his own individuality. He should not surrender his initiative to any social group. There should be no legitimate stopping point short of the absolute. Relative social groupings, such as the state, which claim absolute loyalty, are to be challenged and attacked. The only relationship which is right is the relation of the individual to the ideal.

Thus the social thought of existentialism is not a vacuum, which needs to be filled with an ideology. Rather the social thought of existentialism is critical in the sense that it opposes confusing the partial truth of the social group with the absolute truth of the ideal. It is positive in that it recommends the universal ideal — one might say a medieval unity — in place of partial loyalties to the state, the family, or the fraternal club.

The individual — this is the implication of existentialism for social theory — only may stand in an absolute relation to the absolute.

SUBJECTIVITY: (from the Latin *subjectus,* to bring under, or throw under)

Existentialism is a relativism. The technical term for that relativism is "subjectivity." Subjectivity means that, although objective truth may exist, the individual is too limited by time and circumstance to be certain of ever knowing that objective truth. Therefore, for him, the only truth is subjective, that is, relative to his own ability to discover it. Yet although he cannot know the objective truth, the truth he does know is absolute, that is, the sure and certain foundation on which the individual is to base his decisions and his life.

Furthermore, the very subjectivity of truth has cognitive significance. The fact that existence precedes essence, that life comes before thought, that facts come before definitions, that what appears to be precedes what is, means logically speaking that one individual cannot validly ignore the appearance of things in favor of the essence of things without essentially distorting the nature of existence.

One must begin with things as they appear to be. This means, with reference to the personality, that the emotions should be analyzed, not ignored as "accidental." Thus existentialism has analyzed such emotions as fear and dread, boredom and passion, believing that such an analysis is necessary for the correct understanding of the nature of existence.

Subjectivity, the relativity of truth to the individual, thus exhibits many features which are similar to other forms of contemporary thought, notably the uncertainty principle in physics, in which the physical phenomena are necessarily influenced by the factor of the observer, and the relativity principle.

T

TILLICH, PAUL JOHANNES (1886-1965): Both a philosopher and theologian, Tillich is noted for correlating the questions raised by classical and modern philosophy with the answers provided by theology. To the extent that some of these questions are raised by modern philosophical existentialism, Tillich is correctly classified as an existentialist.

Born in Starzeddel, Brandenburg, on the 20th of August, 1886, his father was a pastor and district superintendent of the Prussian territorial Protestant church. He was impressed with the protected and privileged life which he and his family led.

Studying at Konigsberg, Berlin, Tubingen, Breslau and Halle-Whittenberg, he received the doctor of philosophy degree from Breslau in 1911 and the licentiate in theology from Halle in 1912.

From 1914-1918 he served as a chaplain in the German armed forces. The German soldiers discovered Nietzsche during those years, reading *Thus Spake Zarathustra*. Tillich also remarked that "The belief in special providence died in the trenches," as the discovery was made many times over that a family member could not be spared from the path of an enemy bullet by a special prayer.

After the war he taught at the universities of Berlin, Marburg, Dresden, Leipzig, and Frankfurt-am-Main, where he became professor of philosophy in 1929.

One of the first professors to be forced from his post by the Nazi regime, he came to the United States of America in 1933. He became professor of philosophical theology at Union Theological Seminary in New York City, a post which he held until his retirement in 1955. His major works during this period include *The Protestant Era* (which he wanted to entitle *The End of the*

Protestant Era? but was told by the publisher that no question mark could be in the title), 1948, *The Shaking of the Foundations* (a collection of his sermons), 1948, *The Courage to Be,* 1952, *The New Being* (sermons), 1955, *Love, Power, and Justice,* 1954, *Biblical Religion and the Search for Ultimate Reality,* 1955, *Dynamics of Faith,* 1957.

From 1955 to 1962 he was university professor at Harvard. His major work was his *Systematic Theology* in three volumes, 1951-1963. Some changes in thought are discernable even among the three books in this major work, the most notable being the shift from his statement in the first that God is being-itself, that this is the one non-symbolic statement necessary to get his system going. In the second volume he states that every statement about God, including the one just referred to, is necessarily symbolic. *Theology of Culture* was published in 1959.

In 1962 Tillich became Nuveen professor of theology at the Divinity School of the University of Chicago. *Morality and Beyond,* 1963, and *The Eternal Now* (sermons), also 1963, were published during this period, as was *The Future of Religion,* of which only a small portion is by Tillich.

He died at Chicago on the 22nd of October, 1965. Among the posthumous publications are *Perspectives on 19th and 20th Century Protestant Theology,* 1967, *My Search for Absolutes,* 1967, and *History of Christian Thought,* 1968. In large part these are lecture notes which Tillich would have preferred not to have been published. It remains the case that his major work in every way is the *Systematic Theology.*

BIBLIOGRAPHY

Berdyaev, Nicolas. *Solitude and Society*. Translated by George Reavey. London: The Centenary Press, 1947.
——. *The Destiny of Man*. Translated by Natalie Duddington. London: Geoffrey Bles, 1948.
——. *The Realm of Spirit and the Realm of Ceasar*. Translated by Donald Lowrie, New York: Harper & Brothers. 1952.
Frankl, Viktor E. *From Death-Camp to Existentialism, a Psychiatrist's Path to a New Therapy*. Translated by Ilse Lasch. Boston: Beacon Press, 1959.
Heidegger, Martin: *An Introduction to Metaphysics*. Translated by Ralph Manheim. Garden City, New York: Doubleday & Co., Inc., 1961.
Heidegger, Martin. *Being and Time*. Translated by John Macquarrie and Edward Robinson. New York: Harper & Brothers, 1962.
——. *Discourse on Thinking*. Translated by John M. Anderson and E. Hans Freund. New York: Harper & Row, Publishers.
——. *Existence and Being*. Translated by Werner Brock. Chicago: Henry Regnery Company, 1949.
——. *German Existentialism*. Translated by Dagobert D. Runes. New York: Philosophical Library, 1965.
Jaspers, Karl. *General Psychopathology*. Translated by J. Hoenig and Marian W. Hamilton. Chicago: The University of Chicago Press, 1963.
——. *Philosophy Is for Everyman*. Translated by R. F. C. Hull and Grete Wels. New York: Harcourt, Brace & World, Inc., 1967.
——. *Reason and Anti-reason in Our Time*. Translated by Stanley Godman. London: SCM Press Ltd., 1952.
——. *Reason and Existenz*. Translated by William Earle. The Noonday Press, 1955.
——. *Socrates, Buddha, Confucius, Jesus*. Translated by Ralph Manheim. New York: Harcourt, Brace & World, Inc., 1957.
——. *The European Spirit*. Translated by Ronald Gregor Smith. London: SCM Press Ltd., 1948.
——. *Three Essays*. Translated by Ralph Manheim. New York: Harcourt, Brace & World, Inc., 1964.
——. *Tragedy Is not Enough*. Translated by Harald Reiche, Harry Moore, and Karl Deutsch. Boston: The Beacon Press, 1952.
Kafka, Franz. *The Trial*. Translated by Wilk & Edwin Muir. New York: The Modern Library, 1956.
Kaufmann, Walter. *Existentialism from Dostoevsky to Sartre*. New York: Meridian Books, 1957.
Kierkegaard, Søren. *Attack Upon "Christendom"*. Translated by Walter Lowrie. Boston: The Beacon Press, 1956.
——. *The Concept of Dread*. Translated by Walter Lowrie. Princeton: Princeton University Press, 1957.
——. *The Concept of Irony*. Translated by Lee Capel. New York: Harper & Row, 1965.

————, (Johannes Climacus). *Concluding Unscientific Postscript to the Philosophical Fragments.* Translated by David Swenson and Walter Lowrie. Princeton: Princeton University Press, 1960.

————. *Crisis in the Life of an Actress.* Translated by Stephen D. Crites. New York: Harper & Row, 1967.

————. *The Diary.* Translated by Gerda Andersen. Edited by Peter Rohde. New York: The Philosophical Library, 1960.

————. *Edifying Discourses.* Translated by David and Lillian Swenson. Edited by Paul L. Holmer. New York: Harper & Brothers, 1958.

————, (Victor Eremita). *Either/Or.* Translated by Walter Lowrie. Princeton: Princeton University Press, 1959.

————, (Johannes de Silentio and Anti-Climacus). *Fear and Trembling* and *The Sickness Unto Death.* Translated by Walter Lowrie. Garden City, New York: Doubleday & Co., 1954.

————. *The Gospel of our Sufferings.* Translated by A. S. Aldworth and W. S. Ferrie. Grand Rapids, Michigan: William B. Eerdmans Publishing Company, 1964.

————. *The Journals of Kierkegaard.* Translated by Alexander Dru. New York: Harper & Brothers, 1959.

————. *The Last Years.* Translated and edited by Ronald Gregor Smith. New York and Evanston: Harper & Row, 1965.

————. *On Authority and Revelation.* Translated and edited by Walter Lowrie, New York: Harper & Row, 1966.

————, (Johannes Climacus). *Philosophical Fragments.* Translated by David Swenson. Princeton: Princeton University Press, 1962.

————. *The Point of View for My Work as An Author: A Report to History.* Translated by Walter Lowrie. New York: Harper & Row, 1962.

————. *The Present Age.* Translated by Alexander Dru. New York: Harper & Row, 1962.

————. *Purity of Heart Is To Will One Thing.* Translated by Douglas V. Steere. New York: Harper & Brothers, 1956.

————, (Constantine Constantius). *Repetition, An Essay in Experimental Psychology.* Translated by Walter Lowrie. New York: Harper & Row, 1964.

————. *Samlede Vaerker.* Edited by A. B. Drachmann, J. L. Heiberg, and H. O. Lange. 20 vols. København: Gyldendal, 1962-1964.

————. *Søren Kierkegaards Papirer.* Edited by P. A. Heiberg, V. Khur, and E. Torsten. København: Gyldendalske Boghandel, Nordisk Forlag, 1909-1948.

————, (Hilarius Bookbinder). *All Stages on Life's Way.* Translated by Walter Lowrie. New York: Schocken Books, 1967.

————. *Training in Christianity.* Translated by Walter Lowrie. Princeton: Princeton University Press, 1944.

————. *Works of Love.* Translated by Howard and Edna Hong. New York: Harper & Brothers, 1962.

Kuhn, Roland (ed.). *Existential Psychology.* New York: Random House, 1961.

Marcel, Gabriel. *Homo Viator.* Translated by Emma Craufurd. London: Victor Gollancz Ltd., 1951.

————. *Philosophical Fragments* 1904-1914. Notre Dame, Indiana: University of Notre Dame, 1965.

——. *The Philosophy of Existentialism*. Translated by Manya Harari. New York: The Citadel Press, 1966.

May, Rollo (ed.). *Existence, a New Dimension in Psychiatry and Psychology*. New York: Basic Books Inc., 1958.

——. *Existential Psychology*. New York: Random House, 1961.

Michalson, Carl (ed). *Christianity and the Existentialists*. New York: Charles Scribner's Sons, 1956.

Nietzsche, Friedrich. *Beyond Good and Evil*. Translated by Walter Kaufmann. New York: Random House, Inc., 1966.

——. *The Birth of Tragedy and the Genealogy of Morals*. Translated by Francis Golffing. New York: Doubleday & Company, Inc., 1956.

——. *Thus Spake Zarathustra*. Translated by Thomas Common. New York: The Modern Library, n.d.

Sartre, Jean-Paul. *Being and Nothingness*. Translated by Hazel Barnes. New York: Philosophical Library, 1956.

——. *The Emotions, Outline of a Theory*. New York: Philosophical Library, 1948.

——. *Existentialism*. New York: Philosophical Library, 1947.

——. *Imagination*. University of Michigan, 1962.

——. *Literary and Philosophical Essays*. New York: Philosophical Library, 1957.

——. *Nausea*. Translated by Lloyd Alexander. London: Hamish Hamilton, 1962.

——. *No Exit and The Flies*. New York: Knopf, 1947.

——. *The Philosophy of Existentialism*. Edited by Wade Baskin. New York: Philosophical Library, 1965.

——. *Psychology of Imagination*. New York: Philosophical Library, 1948.

——. *The Reprieve*. New York: Knopf, 1947.

——. *Saint-Genet, Actor and Martyr*. New York: Braziller, 1963.

——. *Search for a Method*. New York: Knopf, 1963.

——. *The Age of Reason*. Translated by Eric Sutton. New York: Alfred A. Knopf, 1959.

——. *Transcendence of the Ego*. New York: Noonday, 1957.

——. *Troubled Sleep*. New York: Knopf, 1951.

——. *The Wall and Other Stories*. New York: New Directions, 1948.

——. *The Words*. New York: Braziller, 1964.

Schilpp, Paul Arthur (ed.). *The Philosophy of Karl Jaspers*. New York: Tudor Publishing Company, 1957.

Tillich, Paul. *Biblical Religion and the Search for Ultimate Reality*. Chicago: The University of Chicago Press, 1955.

——. *Christianity and the Encounter of the World Religions*. New York: Columbia University Press, 1963.

——. *The Courage to Be*. New Haven: Yale University Press, 1952.

——. *Dynamics of Faith*. New York: Harper & Row, 1957.

——. *A History of Christian Thought*. New York: Harper & Row, 1968.

——. *Love, Power, and Justice*. New York: Oxford University Press, 1960.

——. *Morality and Beyond*. New York: Harper & Row, 1963.

——. *My Search for Absolutes*. New York: Simon and Schuster, 1967.

——. *The New Being*. New York: Charles Scribner's Sons, 1955.

————. *The Protestant Era*. Chicago: The University of Chicago Press, 1948.
————. *The Religious Situation*. New York: Meridian Books, 1956.
————. *The Shaking of the Foundations*. New York: Charles Scribner's Sons, 1948.
————. *Systematic Theology*. Chicago: The University of Chicago Press, 1951 (I), 1957 (II), 1963 (III).
————. *Theology of Culture*. New York: Oxford University Press, 1964.